The H.I.M* Book

Also by Chris Fabry

Spiritually Correct Bedtime Stories

Away with the Manger

The 77 Habits of Highly Ineffective Christians

The

H.I.M.*

Book

A
WOMAN'S MANUAL FOR
UNDERSTANDING HER
*HIGHLY IDENTIFIABLE
MALE

Chris Fabry, H.I.M.

WATERBROOK
PRESS

Colorado Springs

THE HIM* BOOK
PUBLISHED BY WATERBROOK PRESS
5446 North Academy Boulevard, Suite 200
Colorado Springs, Colorado 80918
A division of Bantam Doubleday Dell Publishing Group, Inc.

Scripture quotations in this book, unless otherwise noted, are taken from The Holy Bible, New International Version (NIV) © 1973, 1984 by International Bible Society, used by permission of Zondervan Publishing House.

ISBN 1-57856-007-1

© 1997 by Christopher H. Fabry
Published in association with the literary agency of Alive Communications, Inc., 1465 Kelly Johnson Blvd., Suite 320 Colorado Springs, Colorado 80920.

Printed in the United States of America

January 1998—First Edition

1 3 5 7 9 10 8 6 4 2

To Andrea,
the greatest friend a HIM could ever have

Contents

Foreword

Hello, my name is Liz. I am not a HIM, but I'm married to one, gave birth to one, and have dated, known, or worked with zillions of HIMs in my lifetime.

Experience is not the same as understanding, however. That's where Chris Fabry—who really *is* a HIM—will be of service to all of us women who are trying to figure out what makes our men tick.

Hmmm.

Notice we have no companion volume here—*The HER Book*—to educate *men* on what makes *us* tick. Are you kidding? *Who would buy it?* You'd have to purchase it *for* HIM, which turns the whole thing into a homework assignment. HIMs really hate homework. Take my ten-year-old son. Please.

Wait! I'm kidding, of course, which is something Mr. Fabry does exceedingly well here. Chris has an attribute that lots of HIMs do *not* have, which is a sense of humor about HIMself. A real grasp of not only what makes HIM tick, but why the sound of HIM ticking occasionally drives his wife bananas.

The HIM Book has all the thrill of male bashing without the after-guilt *because it was written by a male.*

I love this.

Clearly, the author has spent his therapy dollars well and has come out on top of the self-enlightened heap with his helmet of salvation firmly in place and his breastplate of righteousness strapped on tight. It's Chris's unique view of life as a *Christian* HIM that makes this such a gotta-read-it book.

Think of it as "Dave Barry Goes to Promise Keepers."

For example, thanks to Chris, I finally understand why my own husband, Bill, refuses to hold my purse while I paw through the sale rack at Jacobson's.

What's the big deal? I used to wonder.

Now I get it. When another HIM walks by, the competitive nature of my own HIM gets trampled underfoot. Without a word being said or a punch being thrown, my dear hubby has been deemed "The Loser" because he's standing there with a brown leather purse in his hands.

Wait a minute. *Footballs* are made of brown leather, right?

Ah, but that's not the point. A real HIM doesn't hold purses, or let his wife drive with HIM in the car, or let another guy beat HIM at UNO or any other winner-takes-all game.

Cleverly woven through all the humor in *The HIM Book* (and, girlfriend, I laughed out loud a *bunch*) are genuinely helpful tips for handling life with a HIM. Best I can tell, it can be summed up in three words: *There is hope!*

Yes, there's hope for understanding your very own HIM and for improving your relationship. But it may mean adjusting your expectations.

(If only they knew how low our expectations were to begin with!)

When you get to the part about "most men I know will settle for the Velamint," remember you read it here first: Most women would be *thrilled* with the Velamint and will settle for anything that's not reminiscent of nacho dip or beef jerky. (This will all make sense when you read page 67.)

I hope I've raised your own expectations about his book, dear sister, because it's filled with humor, pathos, and truth. You will read aloud whole portions to your husband, who'll snatch the book out of your hands and say, "Who *is* this guy?"

Chris Fabry is real in a wonderfully scary way. He's a man's man, a guy's guy, (a HIM's HIM?), who willingly invites us to climb inside not only his head, but his heart as well. I didn't expect to cry when I read *The HIM Book*, but I did.

Which means your secret is out, Chris. A nothing-but-a-HIM, dyed-in-the-wool-sports-nut, give-me-the-remote-before-somebody-gets-hurt kinda guy could never have written this book. Chris Fabry, on the other hand, not only understands HIMself, he understands us.

And what woman doesn't delight in that?

Read on without fear, sis. And invest in a pack of Velamints for later.

LIZ CURTIS HIGGS

Author and humorist

Introduction

Hello, my name is Chris. I am a HIM.

I tell you this so you'll understand I have a skewed way of looking at life. It comes with the territory. I don't communicate very well. I shun feelings. I've made work my mistress. I buy affection from my children.

I've written this book exclusively for the woman who wants to understand her husband, fiancé, man, hunk, pal . . . a person referred to hereafter as a HIM. A HIM, or a Highly Identifiable Male, is the man in your life who does certain things, says certain phrases, and acts in ways that, when you hear them described, you can't help but say, "That's him! He does that!"

I am uniquely qualified to give you insight into this person, because I'm an out-of-the-closet HIM. I have been a HIM nearly all my life. (I was a HIM at conception, and I became a Christian HIM at an early age.) I have been friends with HIMs, I've attended church with HIMs, played softball with HIMs, argued, laughed, and once (I think) even got into a deep discussion about the 1972 World Series with a HIM. That was the series between the Cincinnati Reds and Oakland A's, one of the most underrated World Series of the seventies. The Big Red Machine had come through a difficult season battling the Dodgers and had just barely slipped by the Pirates in an incredible bottom-of-the-ninth win at Riverfront Stadium. Roberto Clemente was still playing for Pittsburgh and . . . oh, sorry. Anyway, the conversation would have brought tears to your eyes, believe me.

When I married a few years ago, I was faced with the challenge of communicating all of my HIMness to my wonderful, lovely, yet uninformed, uninitiated wife.* I could tell she didn't understand me by the way her eyes glazed over when I talked about the 1972 World Series and the pitch Catfish Hunter threw Johnny Bench in the bottom of the seventh with two on and two out. (A HIM will correctly tell you the pitcher was Rollie Fingers, and it was the bottom of the eighth, one out.) This was not her fault. She's not a HIM. She had limited close contact with HIMs. How could she know?

Educating her was my goal, but because of my inability to communicate on a deep level (one of my inborn traits), I failed miserably. She doesn't truly understand me. She has no idea what goes on in my mind when she says something like, "How do you feel about that?"

Feel? I think. *What's that?* I have spent my life trying not to feel anything. (Many HIMs are "emotional lepers," a term we'll deal with in this book.)

She was HIM deficient.

What goes on in the mind of a HIM when asked such a question? What happens in a man's brain when he sees his wife crying? What makes a HIM say things like, "Well, if you're going to get all torn up about it, why don't you just cancel the whole thing?" or "Crying's not going to do any good" or "There's no use getting all worked up about it"? We'll explore these and other mysteries concerning the Highly Identifiable Male.

There are many books and myriad experts who can explain why things like this happen. They can give you ten steps to follow and a deep analysis of your problems. I am not a psychologist. I am not a counselor. I am not a pastor or even an associate pastor. I'm not a professor. I have no degree in anything that makes me even remotely qualified to speak in this area except one—I am a HIM.* I am simply a reporter, an observer looking at the process of my own marriage and the marriages of those around me. Therefore, I am here on behalf of your HIM to communicate that he really does love you. In spite of all his HIMness, there beats a heart that desires to please you, that desires to give you happiness and joy unspeakable. I know it's hard to believe, especially the unspeakable part. Trust me.

I am not trying to lump your husband into some category so he can be trashed by feminists. This is one of the big fears of every HIM. I am not broad-brushing all men. All men are not HIMs. I simply want to give you the tools that will help you figure out if your husband is one, and if so, to what degree.

*(Hear me roar.)

3

No matter how entrenched your HIM is, there is still reason for great hope. We're not talking about just any HIM; we're talking about Christian HIMs. There is remarkable potential in the life of a man who is being transformed by the love and power of Jesus Christ.

I see Christian HIMs trying harder than ever before to communicate, to love their wives, and to change in meaningful ways. Take the modern Christian men's movement. Stadiums are now filled with hundreds of thousands of HIMs who listen to speakers, take on the challenge of being committed to their families, and make changes their wives have nagged them about for twenty years.

To appreciate that kind of change in a man's life, you need to understand the way he's wired. So let me take you into the world of the HIM. It's a wonderful place. Much of our life is not in Technicolor but black and white. We live on an even keel, balanced, not too up or down. Hardly ever emotional. Observing the life of a HIM is like riding a roller coaster without the incline. Life goes by really fast, but there's not much to it. And we like to ride alone.

I once had a golfing friend I'll call Dave.* We spent one morning a week in a small group, discussing Patrick Morley's book *Man in the Mirror*. One week we would play golf and talk, the next week we would have breakfast and talk. Some weeks we would have breakfast, golf, and talk. Some weeks we wouldn't talk at all. We'd just stand at the third hole and watch each other hit balls into the water. Some weeks we forgot to show up. We are HIMs.

Because his name is Dave.

Dave was about forty years old, a confirmed bachelor who lived with his dog in an old house. He worked on cars. He loved blaze orange. After a couple of years of playing golf and getting to know each other on a deeper level (like which club to use off the neighbor's carport), we discovered Dave was not only dating a girl from our church named Mary, he was about to wed her! We found this out not from Dave but from an announcement one Sunday morning. My other friend, whose real name is Bob, could not believe that someone we prayed with and shared personal struggles with would say nothing to us about his plans to get married. You would have thought that one day on hole number 8, 5-iron over water, bunker on right (my personal favorite) Dave would have said something like, "Looks like the wind's blowing left to right, Chris. Better aim for the apartment building. And oh, by the way, I'm getting married next week." But he didn't.

When confronted, Dave said, "Well, it just all happened so fast, ha, ha, ha." It was a beautiful wedding, and Dave is now the proud father of three. Things did happen quickly, but Dave remains a HIM through and through.

Of course, not all men are like this. But I'm not talking about all men. I'm talking about HIMs. All HIMs won't exhibit every behavior found in this book. You may have a husband who's able to communicate on a deep level but still treats work as his priority and has a hard time making room for spiritual things. On page 7, I've included a quiz that will help you determine the extent of your man's HIM-ness.

Not everyone will agree with my assessments. Your HIM may look at a chapter and say, "That's not how I think." If he says this, you can be sure he's a HIM. HIMs rarely admit anything.

With a topic this huge, it's impossible to ensure that you'll understand everything about a HIM. But if I can help just one woman appreciate the pitch on a 3-2 count that Johnny Bench took for a called third strike, and not have her eyes glaze over, it'll be worth the effort.

The Ultimate HIM Diagnostic Quiz

Please answer the following questions as true or false.

1. I know more about sea anemones than I do about my husband's feelings.

2. My husband's priorities seem to be work, sports, his car, the yard, church, the kids, and then me.

3. My husband would rather floss with razor wire and gargle shards of glass than discuss our marriage.

4. My husband would rather jam his head on the end of a sharpened pencil than go to counseling.

5. Sometimes I feel alone in this marriage.

6. Okay, I feel alone most of the time in this marriage.

7. I can't tell you how alone I feel in this marriage.

8. I really wish my husband would significantly change in a couple of areas.

9. My husband is a great person and I love him, but I'm frustrated because we don't seem to be on the same team.

10. I am willing to do just about anything to change our relationship for the better.

If you answered five or more questions as "true," you are married to a HIM.

There is a great deal of human nature in man.

CHARLES KINGSLEY

All the world's a stage,
And all the men and women merely players.

WILLIAM SHAKESPEARE

That is the happiest conversation where there
is no competition, no vanity,
but a calm quiet interchange of sentiments.

SAMUEL JOHNSON

Chapter One

HIMs Think Life Is One Big Competition

My wife Andrea and I were having dinner with a couple of very spiritual people. They were headed toward the mission field and a life of service to God. They were *really* spiritual. They had a "call" and were working every day to realize their goal of going into a foreign country that was way too hot, had no running water or electricity, and worst of all, no cable TV.

We finished our dinner and were sitting around talking about spiritual things, when someone innocently said, "Let's play a game."

The wives giggled with excitement. To them a game meant fun and fellowship. I knew better. In the mind of a HIM there is no such thing as a game just for fellowship. When the word *game* is even mentioned, a sharp minor chord sounds in a HIM's ears like the first four notes in Beethoven's Fifth Symphony. Testosterone flows. Muscles tighten. He reaches for his mental athletic supporter.

The women were going to laugh and talk and enjoy each other. They were ready to "play." For them a game was simply another way to enjoy their relationship. But my friend and I immediately began thinking of the battle. We weren't going to "play" anything. We were going to war. As a true HIM, I didn't care how far away these people were moving, this was my chance—possibly my last—to compete.

The methods of weaponry were meager: Scrabble, Rook, perhaps a quick round of Parcheesi. Then I heard a faint voice say, "How about UNO?" And thus began the longest night of our lives—or close to it.

My friend's wife won the first game. My wife took the second in record time. My friend's wife won the third.

I was able to control my competitive juices by telling myself, "This is UNO. This is not a competition." However, my good friend, this godly tower of spiritual strength, was turning red. His fingers and eyes twitched. His concentration got more intense. The fact that this was UNO, a simple game, only made it worse for him.

"Draw Four," his wife said.

"Draw Four?!?" he said incredulously, slamming his cards on the table. "How come I always get the lousy Draw Four cards?"

"Oh honey, you don't get all of them," his wife said. "I got one last time, and I was fine with it."

His eyes darted from player to player. *No friends here*, he must have thought. He flicked a glance at his cards like a hungry lion drooling in the grass. He sized up his prey. Should he play the Wild card or the Reverse? He waved his hand nervously by his side like a gunfighter. But on the very next play, all that his macho moves netted him were another Draw Four and two Reverses that took the game out of his control. He was on UNO Island, a player unto himself. Lonely. Pensive.

Finally the play reversed to my friend, but before he could put his card down, I heard his wife say with a certain knowing glee, "UNO!" She had but one card left.

"Uno?!?!?" my friend said, the bile of competition rising from the depths of his inner HIMness. "How does that happen? How do you do that? That's not fair! I quit. This is a stupid game."

How can anyone compete at UNO, I ask you? It's just a game, right? Well, I asked that of another couple a few years later, and the husband looked at me with chagrin.

"There's a method to winning," he said. "I'll show you."

We played three more games. He won all three. Then he smiled as if to say, "I told you."

It doesn't matter where he is or what he's doing, a true HIM will find a way to compete. If no one else is around, he competes with himself. How many times have you come home to discover your HIM preparing to take a shower but stuck near the clothes hamper, trying to flip his underwear into it with his toe?* Have you ever wondered why it takes us so long in the bathroom? We time bodily functions. It's all a competition.

Counselors now know that most HIMs suffer from what is

---

*(Maybe I'm the only one who has ever done this, but I swear it happens a lot.)

clinically known as "HIM Competitive Syndrome," or HIMCOS. This is much like PTSD—post-traumatic stress disorder—except HIMs don't have to be in a war or live through a plane crash to get it. All they have to do is be a HIM, and it comes naturally.

HIMs compete over who has the latest and best computer hardware and software. They compete over the strength of their coffee and how long they grind their coffee beans. They compete over sports minutiae. They compete by stumping their friends with film dialogue or song lyrics no one should remember. HIMs even compete with their kids.

HIMSPEAK

"I'm not going to play on the church softball team this year."
Translation: I'm tired of competing with my pastor for the most RBIs.

When my children were young, they kept pestering me to play Candyland. I hated the thought. I finally saw how much it meant to them, so I sat down on the floor, chose my blue playing piece, shuffled the cards, and away we went. It wasn't long until I was into the game, trying to hit the spaces where I could advance quickly. I wanted Queen Frostine; I salivated over her beauty. But I kept getting Plumpy and Grandma Nut, who are not so far along on the game board and not half as pleasing to view. When my daughter passed the last square before I did, ready to go into that blessed happiness of chocolate delight, I did not feel joy for her. I did not pat her three-year-old back and say, "Good job; you did that very well." I simply said, "Let's play it again. But this time Dad gets to go first."

Competition is one of the most pronounced traits of a HIM. It's the driving force in a HIM's life—to be better than someone else; to compare his abilities with someone else's abilities; to show everyone, especially himself, that he has worth.

The disease—HIMCOS—permeates nearly every part of a HIM's life. A HIM competes when he drives the car. You will rarely, if ever, see a HIM riding in the passenger seat with his wife behind the wheel. It's too painful. It means he has no control. Your HIM may well go crazy if you insist on driving more than once a month.

A HIM competes for parking spaces; he will drive through each lane of the parking lot to find the closest parking spot to the grocery store.

A HIM competes for lanes on the expressway. Things are fine as long as traffic around him stays polite; but let someone cut him off just once and watch what happens. If a woman gets cut off in traffic, she'll turn to her passengers and say, "Did you see that? Can you be-lieve the way people drive? Somebody's going to teach that guy a les-son some day." A HIM's response? "Watch this! I'm gonna teach this guy a lesson!" He then proceeds to pull up beside the other driver to bawl him out with a glaring look, then shakes his head and drives off even faster.

A Christian HIM is at a disadvantage here, because he can't make any of the creative gestures other drivers make. He can throw his hands up in the air or smack the dashboard, but he can't yell obscenities or wave offensive signals at other drivers. This is really the only drawback to being a Christian HIM. He can't vent anger creatively, he must turn the other cheek—or fender—if he has to.

I recall one such competitive situation, when I was driving alone and got cut off. I resisted the urge to compete with the other car and tried to get my HIMness under control. However, a little later, a window in the car rolled down, and onto my windshield flew a hamburger wrapper, a soda cup, and an empty paper bag. I was outraged. I couldn't believe anyone would be so callous and inconsiderate. But I didn't just shake my head and pledge not to be a litterbug. I had to do something. I had to compete.

I pulled into the right lane and sped up. In seconds I was beside the offending driver with my window rolled down. "Stop throwing out trash!" I yelled, mouthing the words dramatically.

The passenger in the car, a grizzled man with a mustache, rolled his window down as well. "What did you say?"

With even more exaggerated outrage, I yelled, "I said, stop throwing trash out of your window!"

He turned to the driver and said something. The driver looked over at me and said something back to the passenger, who again turned to me. He gave me a sick smile and, with great wryness, he slowly and even more dramatically replied, "Thank you, officer."

In the pit of my stomach I knew I had lost the competition, defeated by a sardonic litterer. This proves again that a HIM will go to unimaginable lengths to compete. No one in his right mind would say anything to anyone on the roadways these days. There's too much danger involved. But a HIM with a competitive heart will wade into any situation.

You're probably wondering when a HIM contracts HIMCOS. The disease germinates at the very moment of conception. Scientists are now able to record the earliest sounds inside the fertilized egg. With a microphone the size of gnat dandruff, these brilliant men, who competed over who could make the smallest microphone, can now let us hear exactly what happens immediately after the sperm penetrates the wall of the egg.

Here, for the first time in written form, because nobody else would have believed it, is a transcript of what the sperm actually says.*

> "Whee, I'm through, I'm through! I made it! I
> was the only one! Whee! Nice try guys, but I'm
> number one today!! Somebody give me a

*(With gratitude to Helmut von Spielganger, who translated the text from Spermese to English.)

high-five. Oh, wait, I'm the only one who made

it. Whee! I'm number one. I'm number one!"

As the baby HIM develops, he begins the process of what will become a life filled with competition. Skip forward with me a few years and see the effects of this genetic phenomenon. Little Jimmy has been asked to play at little Billy's house for the very first time. Billy's mother asked Jimmy's mother if he could come over, because the fathers of Billy and Jimmy are simply not competent to make such a decision. (Actually, both fathers were out playing golf for $5 a hole.) Here is a brief portion of the boys' initial conversation.

Jimmy: Are these your toys?

Billy: Yes.

Jimmy: I've got more than that.

Billy: So? Mine are newer than yours.

Jimmy: Are not!

Billy: Are too!

Jimmy: Well, you have cheesy teeth.

Billy: Do not!

Jimmy: Do too!

Billy: My dad can beat up your dad.

Jimmy: Cannot!

Billy: Can too! My mom can even beat up your dad.

Jimmy: Cannot!

Billy: Can too!!

All competition invariably leads to this basic point—the ability of one father to physically best the other father. There are many theories as to why this happens, but the truth is this: At bedtime, when you think your HIM is tucking your son in or saying prayers with him, he's actually instilling unhealthy societal thoughts in his mind.

Daddy: Jimmy, are you ready for bed?

Jimmy: Yes, Daddy.

Daddy: Did you get dressed quicker than your sister?

Jimmy: Yes, Daddy.

Daddy: How long did it take you to go to the bathroom?

Jimmy: Forty-five seconds.

Daddy: Good. You know it takes girls longer, don't you?

Jimmy: Yes, Daddy.

Daddy: Well, are you ready for the most important part of the day?

Jimmy: You mean, when we say our prayers together?

Daddy: Well, yes, but also when I tell you all the people I can beat up.

Jimmy: Oh, yeah. Go ahead.

Daddy: Well, let's see. I can beat up Billy's dad. And I can beat up Tommy's dad. And you know that new boy who moved in across the street?

Jimmy: The one I beat in the footrace today?

Daddy: Yep, that's the one. I can beat up his dad, too.

Jimmy: Wow, that's great! You can beat up just about every-body.

Daddy: I know, Son. Shall we pray?

Jimmy: Dad, can you pray tonight instead of me?

Daddy: Sure, Son. Heavenly Father, I want to thank you tonight for Jimmy. Thank you that he's such a good boy. Help him get lots of rest tonight so he can wake up tomorrow and prove he's better than everybody else, except me, of course. And help him to know that you love him unconditionally. Amen.

By the time Jimmy moves on to high school, his penchant for competition is second nature. He approaches typing, science, and history the same way he approaches basketball, baseball, and getting his locker open. He must be first. When he reaches college, his desire is more focused. There are smaller areas of competition. Instead of competing with the whole school, he's competing in one department, but his drive and intensity continue to increase.

Through sports, school, and everyday life, HIMCOS builds until the child is ready to consider the opposite sex. Dating brings with it the ultimate competition. Who will get the prettiest girl? Which boy will gain the affection of the most desirable female on campus? This, of course, leads to behavior that is uncharacteristic of the HIM. He talks. He listens. He is thoughtful. He woos. A HIM loses interest in romance when there's simply no competition. Who wants to play a game when there's no definable winner? Romance within marriage is no fun, because there's no loser. Your HIM will never admit this, but it's true.

Believe it or not, a HIM will even turn his faith into a competition. I'm positive a HIM came up with the "Sword Drill" and the concept of memorizing verses for competition. So was the person who first suggested the Sunday school attendance competition between churches. And the person had to be a HIM who said, "Hey, why don't we start a softball league between churches?"

If you want an indicator of how far Christian HIMs can take competition, you need look no further than the softball diamond on a summer evening. Pastor Smith and Pastor Jones meet at the center of the field and shake hands as First Baptist meets Second Presbyterian. While they're leading the spectators in a word of prayer, Deacon Brown from the Baptists and Elder White from the Presbyterians are going through their motivational techniques in their respective dugouts.

> *Pastor Smith* (on microphone): Thank you for allowing us to meet here, for the beauty of your creation and the joy of sport. . . .
>
> *Deacon Brown* (in dugout): Now men, we're here for one reason. Sure, we want to have fun and we want to act friendly and all that. But the main reason we're here is to win!
>
> *Team* (subdued): Yeah!
>
> *Elder White* (in dugout): . . . and I want to be nice and friendly as much as the next fellow, but these Baptists mean business. They're not here to give us the right hand of fellowship.

They're gonna hit the ball over our heads and basically try to run us right out of this park. So we've gotta get men on. We've gotta take a few balls so we get a few walks, and then pow—homerun!

Team (less subdued): Yeah!

Pastor Jones (on microphone): . . . we pray that you will keep all our players healthy today, that you will keep them from injury, that you will protect them from harm from other players or from overestimating their abilities like Hank did last week. We pray for Hank's hamstring and ask that you give the doctors wisdom.

Deacon Brown: I've heard there are some here who say they want to play just to have fun. Well, I have just one thing to say about that . . .

Elder White: . . . it's a lot more fun to win than lose, so let's get out there and have fun! Fight, fight, fight!!!

Pastor Jones: In Jesus' name, Amen.

The game that immediately follows doesn't resemble a church outing as much as a battle scene from the Old Testament. The only thing missing is the pillaging and beheading. Men become boys at church softball games. They high-five each other when they're winning and sit on the bench and blame each other when they're losing. If God had meant for Christians to play softball together, I believe he would have webbed a deep well-pocket into our left hands!

Soon after my wife and I went to counseling*, I began to see how I was caught in a vicious downward spiral of competition. I competed with her at parenting tasks. Could I diaper faster and with more precision? I competed at driving the car. I competed at being nicer to my in-laws. When I began to see the problem of my competitive spirit, I competed over who was getting healthier faster. I claimed that I had a better handle on the issue of competition, thereby nullifying my claim. That realization was a bitter defeat, but I did realize it first.

I don't think women are naturally competitive. If a woman is, it comes from years of being around a competitive HIM. She has to compete to defend herself.

H I M S P E A K

"You always . . ."
Translation: Come on, come on, I dare ya . . .

When I looked at my own problem, I started noticing the habits of other couples. The husband would make a statement such as, "Our first house cost $40,000." The wife then corrected him. The rest of us didn't care whether it was $37,500 or $40,000, but that

I talk about this more in Chapter 7.

doesn't matter to competing couples. For them, the smaller the issue, the bigger the competition.

This type of behavior is most damaging to friends who have to sit and listen to the mind-numbing chatter. See how long it takes you to read the following without becoming annoyed enough to hit something.

"Oh, Bob, tell the story about how we met."

"No, they've heard that before, haven't they?"

"No, they haven't, Bob. Go ahead and tell it."

"Karla, they don't want to hear that again. I've told it to them at least forty times."

"No more than twelve. Now come on; this is really good."

"All right. Well, my little sister was—

"Becky—that's his little sister . . ."

"Yeah, Becky was in the hospital for some kind of surgery or something . . ."

"She went in for a bad kidney infection, and they found out she had appendicitis. Poor thing."

". . . so Becky was having her appendix out when Karla came in to—"

"No, Bob, she wasn't having her appendix out just then; that wasn't until later. I was there to take down the information to fill out her chart."

"Right. Okay. So Karla was taking down this information about Becky, and Karla asked if she had any brothers or sisters, and Becky said she had an older brother. So my mother came in and—"

"Oh! You left out the best part!"

"What part was that?"

"The part where I ask Becky if you're cute. See, Becky said she had an older brother, and I automatically asked her if he was cute, just as a joke. So then his mother came in and showed me a picture of him. Go ahead now, you tell it."

"So my mother showed her a picture of me from high school and—"

"No, it was your freshman college picture. . . ."

Be honest now. At some point in the above conversation you wanted to stand up and scream, *"Stop it!!! Just let him tell the story!!!"* This is the insidious thing about competition. It reveals itself in small ways that the perpetrators don't even realize.

But there's one form of verbal jousting the wife of a HIM generally doesn't understand. Call it fighting, call it conflict, call it disagreement. I've known couples who actually fight over what to name it. Whatever the term, you see this break in the relationship quite differently than your HIM does, and it's the direct result of years of competition. I'll give you an example of what I mean.

Let's say the situation concerns getting a baby-sitter and eating dinner out. You're thinking that you always take care of the details. You call the sitter, you give the instructions, you change the diapers, you mentally prepare the children for the evening, then you get dressed and ready for dinner. You do all this while your HIM clicks through television channels or reads the paper or opens the mail. So this time, when you bring up the idea of going out to eat, you have in mind something totally different. A scenario of shared responsibility—the way marriage ought to be.

"I was thinking we could go out to eat tonight, since it's been a while," you say.

"Huh?" he says, shuffling the mail, not paying attention.

"I was thinking we'd burn the house down, get the insurance money, and *go out to dinner tonight.*"

"Oh yeah, sure. Sounds good."

You walk out of the room knowing that the very act of not calling the sitter will bring about an undesirable scene, but you decide the principle is worth it. About five minutes before time of departure, your HIM stands, puts the mail on the shelf, and runs to get dressed. When he returns, he says in a bewildered tone, "Where's the sitter?"

"What do you mean, where's the sitter," you say. "I wanted you to get the sitter."

"But you always get the sitter."

"I know. That's why I didn't want to get the sitter this time."

"But I don't have a relationship with the sitter like you do."

"You don't have a relationship with the sitter because you've never remembered her name."

"Well, it's not like I've never gotten a sitter before. I do it sometimes."

"When? When was the last time you called and got a sitter?"

"You know I can't remember things like you can."

"I'll tell you. Three years ago when you wanted to go see *The Potato That Ate L.A.*, and I said I wouldn't go unless you got the sitter."

This is the preliminary joust to the real match coming only moments later. Let me help you understand what's going on inside your HIM. For you, there's hurt, anger, a sense of abandonment, shirked responsibility, and a general disdain for the thoughtlessness of your HIM. But in his mind, inside that vast cavernous gray matter, your HIM thinks one thing: competition!

H I M S P E A K

"Well, you may be right, but . . ." Translation: You won the first round. Care for two out of three?

You see, when you get upset about something, your husband isn't trying to understand the depth of your pain. It doesn't occur to him that he hasn't taken responsibility or has, in any way, been thoughtless. You think he's abandoned you. But the first thing that pops into his mind is, *How can I win this?* His initial mental energy regarding this conflict has nothing to do with analyzing the situation and coming up with a solution. He views you as the competition, and he will do anything to make sure he comes out on top.

If you're like most women, this is incomprehensible. You can't imagine how anyone can be so devoid of feeling and common sense. But your HIM has been living this way all his life. His motto is, "When there's conflict, compete!" If he wins the argument, he's safe. If he loses, which rarely happens, he pouts or acts like nothing happened.

I'm going to tell you a great HIM secret. Do not miss this. If, when you have conflict, you can get your HIM to see that you are not trying to win an argument, you have a better chance at resolution. If you can help your HIM understand that this problem is one in a pattern of things that have built up, you may be able to break through and help him overcome the dreaded HIMCOS.

As long as there have been men, there has been competition. It began in the Garden. Things were perfect. No clothes. No shame. No voice mail. Then Adam and Eve sinned, and the whole earth was filled with the need to prove itself.

What happened to the first two brothers in the world? Cain killed Abel because Abel's offering was better.

Why do you think Methuselah lived till he was 969? Somebody bet him he couldn't make it past 850! Boy, he showed him.

Think about Noah's story. We know that God told him exactly how to build the ark, and there were many wicked people who came out and mocked him. How did he hold up under such pressure? I think deep in Noah's heart he knew nobody was going to build a bigger boat.

Jacob competed with Esau. Laban competed with Jacob and gave him the wrong wife. Joseph competed with his brothers and nearly got killed. Moses competed with Pharaoh and did that really neat snake trick with his staff. The Israelites competed with Moses. Joshua judges Ruth. (Sorry.) Samson competed with the Philistines. Actually, Samson competed with everybody and finally brought the whole house down! Saul competed with David. David's sons competed with him. The disciples competed with each other over who would be the greatest in the kingdom. On and on it goes.

Competition is at the heart of conflicts between men and women. HIMs have never been able to understand why their wives put a priority on relationship instead of winning. While you live a well-rounded existence, balancing feelings, friends, spouse, children, work, play, and spirituality, your HIM does nothing but punt, pass, and kick.

Here's what you should do to stem the tide of rivalry. Try not to put yourself in the position of one-on-one competition. If you're at a party, try to team up with your husband and work together. Be aware of the symptoms of HIMCOS: clenched teeth, a wild, boyish attitude. When you sense competition running full force through his veins, quickly run an errand.

When you're in the midst of a heated argument with your HIM, clarify that you're not trying to win; you don't need to come out on top in this argument. You simply want to get at the truth. This is the antidote to competition in conflict. The truth will set you both free.

If you will be patient with your HIM, he may realize this on his own and desire to change. But if you try to tell him this, he will simply compete with you and tell you about all your problems. Avoid this cycle at all costs.

What You Can Do

1. Learn to channel your HIM's competitive spirit and have it work for you. For example, if you have numerous household chores to do, and he's sitting around reading the paper, involve him. Say, "Honey, I folded these clothes as fast as I could last week and I came up with twenty-two minutes. I bet you can't top that."

2. Invest in a good stopwatch.

3. Realize how difficult it is for your HIM to overcome his addiction to competition. When he shows any improvement—when he loses at Scrabble and doesn't put his fist through the wall; when he picks up the "Q" and doesn't spike it on the kitchen table— verbally affirm how much you appreciate his working on his competitiveness.

4. Discuss competition with your HIM, and if he does admit that he may have a problem in this area, come up with a strategy to help him. I suggest you wear a striped shirt around the house, and every time you feel he's competing with you or the kids, blow a whistle or throw a flag. Three infractions and he must vacuum. Technicals are two loads of laundry.

The more I see of man, the more I like dogs.

He who finds a wife finds a good thing.

Next to God, we are indebted to women, first for life itself, and then for making it worth having.

Chapter Two

HIMs Take Everything You Do for Granted

O n behalf of all HIMs, I dedicate this chapter to women whose tireless work around the home goes unnoticed. This is what your HIM wants to communicate to you but just hasn't figured out yet. This allegory is about a pilgrim of sorts, who becomes his wife for a day.

The Husband's Progress

As I drove through the expressways of this world, hurrying on my way to work, I lighted on a certain rest area, where I parked and drifted off to sleep. As I slept, I dreamed a dream.

I dreamed, and behold, I beheld myself changed, with long hair, a shapely figure, and a feeling that I was on duty twenty-four hours a day. I beheld myself (but it was actually my wife), and boy, was I tired.

It was still dark, and I was cradling our infant son, who was coughing and making all kinds of rude noises in the night. Another body stirred beside me, but I said, "It's okay; go back to sleep. I'll take care of the baby." And I did care for him, there in the darkness, with no one to thank me, no one to remember my sacrifice.

I comforted the child with persistent "Shhs" and a loving pat no one saw, for no one was awake except me and the screaming child, and behold, he did stink. It was in the stillness of the night, with the coughing and sputtering, and a quick snap of adhesive on a new diaper, that I felt my lips move in prayer for this little one and for each precious life under my care. And then I sang, sweetly, gently, and the child in my arms rolled his eyes back and gave up the fight. He lay there on my chest until I stood to lay him down. But he woke again, and I was up the rest of the night with this sleeping lump on top of me. Strangely enough, I didn't mind.

As the sun rose, I looked, and behold, I saw all the duties for the day listed under the refrigerator magnet. I saw other things not listed that no one would do if I didn't, such as diaper changes too numerous to mention, laundry to be picked up, sorted, washed, dried, sorted, folded, and placed again in respective chambers. I saw dirty dishes, empty lunch pails, report cards to sign, and notes to teachers waiting to be stuffed in backpacks. I saw coats and hats and scarves and gloves flying from a box near the doorway as my children scrambled out the door.

In the midst of these duties, I saw tenderness. My child made a mess on the kitchen table of brown sugar, microwaved marshmallows, and cat food. (Don't ask about this one. I'm still trying to figure it out.) I took her by the hand, and instead of scolding her, I cleaned her up and brought out Play-Doh. Then I took a moment to stand in the corner and watch her play. After lunch I bent down on that floor and picked up all the Play-Doh, that is, all the Play-Doh that was not ground into the tile. I found a few peas and Cheerios, too. Instead of complaining, I thought about the day when I would long for the chore of scraping Play-Doh and chasing dried peas across the kitchen floor and into the heating vent. I brushed back a tear.

As I looked at this scene, I was thinking all the while that this was not the way I would do it. But there I was, doing all these things in my dream, with my shapely figure, and still feeling like I was on duty twenty-four hours a day. (I cannot stress this enough.)

When the wee ones were napping, I didn't fritter away my time in any way. There were books and magazines to read, and TV soaps to watch, but I spent a few minutes reading the Bible and then went to work at the small business I had begun for the purpose of bringing in some extra income for the family. I returned phone calls and faxes, and opened the mail. There were bills to pay, invoices to write, and paperwork to file.

Soon, my older children came home, and I felt like a coat tree as they clung to me like koalas. They each told me things about their day that I had never heard before, because you just don't tell those types of things to fathers. But they were telling me, and the experience was a blessed revelation.

While I busied myself about the kitchen, getting snacks, cleaning spills, and answering homework questions, my husband arrived. He had sort of a kingly presence about him, as if we were all supposed to fall down at his feet and bring an offering. But I kissed him sweetly and welcomed him home and talked about his day as if all the things I had done were of no importance.

Oh, you should have heard the things he thought were important! The children were growing up before his eyes, and he didn't even notice it; but I bit my tongue and prayed he would soon discover this fact.

I felt tired, but there was no respite. I took the baby to the doctor and dragged the rest of the troops along so my husband could "get a little work done." When I came back from the pharmacy with an armload of medicine and the whining masses, he sat on the couch, still in his work clothes, reading the paper. The shelf I had asked him to put up three months ago stood in the corner of the closet. This is the same closet that has no door on it because the screws are stripped and the door now stands in the laundry room.

The vacuum cleaner also stood like a lonely soldier by the couch, and I wondered why he hadn't fixed the little rattle that now sounds like a Howitzer every time we turn the thing on.

I realized he didn't understand when he spoke to me in a not-so-pleasant voice.

"Where did you go?" he asked. "You had three calls."

I thought I would have a coronary right then and there, and

probably would have if I weren't in this other person's shoes. But I quietly explained and then organized the medicine so any animal with a brain the size of a chestnut would be able to dole out the correct dosages. Then I prepared dinner and put it on the table.

After dinner I gave the baby a bath and once again picked up clothes, toys, shoes, and books. I asked my husband to dispense the different medication while I prepared the vaporizers for each room. I felt a bit angry the third time he asked how much each child should get, but again, I bit my tongue and gave him detailed information.

When, at last, I laid my weary body in the bed, after brushing and flossing, of course, I felt something strange on my shoulder and was startled to find my husband's hand there and him saying in a rather breathless voice, "Hello." This was the voice of passion.

Behold, I yelped, for I could not understand how one person could plumb such depths of insensitivity. My yelp then woke the sickest child, who again slumbered on my chest through the night while my husband snored and my children breathed the vaporized air. What surprised me most was the depth to which I would serve, with little thanks and no pay.

I heard a honking sound, and immediately I awoke from my dream at the rest area. I saw that I was late for a meeting, and I rushed to be on time. Before I went into the conference room, I stopped by a phone and dialed the familiar number.

The ringing ceased, and I heard the congested cry of a small child, and a pleasant voice said, "Hello?"

"Hi, it's me," I said, emotion welling up within me.

"Oh, hi!" she said, and my heart felt like I had just hit a triple to right field. I wanted to tell her about my dream and all the things I had learned—the ways I had been insensitive to her, the demanding things I had no reason or right to demand. The ways I had let her down and failed to pick up my share of the work at home.

"I just wanted to say . . ." I said, faltering.

"You wanted to say what?"

"Well . . . uh . . . I wanted to call before I went into this meeting and say . . ."

"Yes?"

"I—I wanted to ask what we're having for dinner tonight."

She paused for a moment, and a little piece of me died holding that phone. There was a tiny bit of pain in her voice that I would never have noticed had I not dreamt about her life.

"Chicken," she finally said. "I think chicken and rice, with that seasoning the children like."

"That sounds great," I said. "I'll try to be home early."

"Oh?"

"Yeah. Maybe I can feed the kids dinner and let you go out with one of your friends. Would you like that?"

She didn't say anything. I thought she might need a defibrillator, but in a moment she caught her breath and managed to choke out, "That would be great, honey. That would be so great."

I hung up the phone and headed into the meeting. As I sat down and put my notes in order, I straightened my tie and noticed a small red stain on the pocket of my shirt. It looked very much like cherry-flavored children's aspirin, and I paused there in the conference room at the office and prayed. I asked God to never again let me take my wife for granted. I asked him to give me the strength to give her that night off. And I prayed that I would never again assume that it's her duty to get the kids dressed for church on Sunday.

This is a very nice story with one problem: In real life everybody doesn't live happily ever after.* Something deep inside your HIM keeps him from connecting with your feelings. It tells him that if he does connect with you, he will then be expected to connect with you next time. It means he'll have to work at this thing called relationship. He fears he'll have to move his fingers in quotation marks for the rest of his life as he says words like "connect." (Oh no, it's happening to me. Maybe it's a "full" moon.)

I speak with women all the time whose husbands simply don't understand what they go through each day. Actually, I don't speak with women all the time, but I do speak with my wife, Andrea, and she talks to women all the time whose husbands don't understand. Then she tells me about it, so I feel like I've spoken with these women, even though it was only my wife who spoke with them.

These women say their HIMs work all day in an office environment, or at a shop or a plant, and when they get home, they don't realize the importance of the home to the wife. The men don't

*Sometimes Mom does lose it with the children.

understand it's vital for a HIM to regard his wife's space as valid and valuable.

"I'm going to take more responsibility around the house."
Translation: I will show up for dinner on time tonight.

How many times have I heard my wife talk about this? Plenty, because she keeps telling me that I don't value the home like she does. Okay, so I was lying about all the women she talks to. She does have a lot of friends, but the person who doesn't really value her space is me, and I'm owning up to it now. (I hope you're happy, dear.)

Here's what I understand of her "pain." (There go the quotation marks again.) She thinks that if I spent my whole workday in our living room, with the thin carpet and the vacuum that rattles, looking at the hole in the wall by the couch, I'd want something done so that my work environment would be more livable. If I had to do dishes every day, knowing that one more visit from the repairman would fix the dishwasher, and that all I needed to fix the light switch was a seventy-nine-cent piece of plastic from the hardware store, I would put a much higher priority on getting those things fixed around the house.

But you know what? I don't live in my home office every day. And if I did, I'd just move the couch to cover up the hole in the wall.

But that's my penchant for fixing everything, which she says she doesn't want me to do. Do you see what it's like to live as a HIM? We're told, when the emotions start to flow, that we're not supposed to fix everything, we're just supposed to listen. Then, when there's a hole in the wall or the light doesn't work, we're all of a sudden supposed to act and not listen anymore. It's enough to make you want to put another hole in the wall.

My wife often complains about my lack of involvement in the house, and it's usually after I've been in my home office a long time on the weekend and haven't changed any diapers, and I've let the dishes pile up until they look like Mount Everest. But this is my way. I like a challenge, even when it comes to dishes. I like to pretend I'm scaling this mountain of dishes, fighting off the bitterly cold temperatures, risking life and limb just for the satisfaction of knowing I made it to the top. The same goes with diapers. I like a challenge.

She thinks I'm crazy or lazy or both.

She's right, of course. I don't think of the home in the same way she does. When she had me paint our bedroom pink and put all the floral swags on the wall and the brass-coated flowers over the head of our bed, I did it. But I hardly notice them when I walk in the room today. I did notice last year when one of those lead flowers fell down and knocked me in the head one night. And when she threatened to throw away my favorite shirt with all the holes in the back of it, I nearly fell apart with grief. I care for that shirt, not the lead flowers.

I see our house and think, *Aaah, we still have a roof, and the walls are standing. It's a home.* But I'm a HIM. My wife looks at our house and sees nothing but the fluorescent light over the kitchen table that doesn't work when she flips the switch. You have to stand there and pump it a few times, and the sides have fallen apart and are held together with duct tape, but a light isn't that important to me, especially when I can try to turn the light on in three less pumps than she can.

If you were to think like a HIM for even twenty-four hours, testosterone flowing, sports metaphors clanging about your head, and all those powers of concentration focused on finding the perfect power tool or just the right setting on the hot water heater, you would understand why your HIM takes everything you do for granted.

It's not that he doesn't appreciate what you do. He does. But no matter what your particular duties are, whether you're a full-time mom or a full-time mom with a job outside the home, he hasn't figured out that you need to be told you're appreciated more than once in a lifetime. A HIM looks at a woman doing work around the home and figures she must really enjoy it. Why else would she spend that much time doing it?

A friend of my wife recently said about her HIM, "He doesn't take any responsibility around the home, so I take it, and then I'm seen as a bad person for being controlling and rigid. Have your husband explain that in his book."

Well, my friend, if I could explain that in my book, I would not only be richer than Microsoft's Bill Gates, I would no doubt be a king on some remote island. Now that I think about it, this describes Bill Gates, except his island isn't remote.

If you're feeling like your HIM doesn't carry his share of the load around the home, I advise you to analyze your expectations. Does your HIM really not get involved around the house, or does he just not do the things you want him to do? Does he take care of the trash and the car and the gutters and the lawn? Many women take these things for granted, like a HIM is supposed to enjoy mowing the lawn. It's just not true, and our inner HIMs are crying out to be noticed.

Does he get the paper in the morning? (This is a very difficult job. You have no idea what a strain it is on a HIM to get the paper and read it.)

HIMSPEAK

"What were you planning for dinner?" Translation: I don't like what you're planning for dinner.

Maybe he doesn't wash the dishes, because he knows you'll come along later and do them. Or rewash them correctly. Maybe he doesn't vacuum or make the bed, because he knows it won't be right. Believe me, this puts a dent in a HIM's ego. I should know. Andrea frequently rewashes the dishes, simply because she finds a little cheese stuck to the plates. I ask you, is a ketchup stain worth hurting your HIM's self-esteem? When I attempt to make the bed, it seems I never do it right. The corners aren't tucked firmly enough, and it's too lumpy for her tastes. She'll come along later and fluff the pillows and rearrange them, so why bother?

This, of course, is a cop-out and would hold no water in a court of law, but it seems quite rational to a HIM, because he hates doing dishes, vacuuming, and making the bed.

When he's done a subpar job, your HIM will no doubt say something like, "You have this impossible standard I can never live up to." You must learn the language of your husband. In HIMSPEAK this should be translated, "I didn't want to do it in the first place, so why don't you just do it."

If, after analyzing your expectations, you still believe your HIM doesn't carry his full share around the house, I have three suggestions for you. First, take every opportunity to let him know how important your home is to you.

As a HIM, I don't understand what my wife thinks as she walks into our home. I will never understand why it's so important for her to have every bed made, every room spotless, and all the shelves in the refrigerator empty when we go on vacation. I will never comprehend that look of disbelief when she glances at my side of the closet, or when she watches me wad my pants into the size of a Ping-Pong ball and throw them into the corner. My wife is a wonder to behold when she gets in her cleaning mode. She looks like the Tasmanian Devil with a duster, and I love her for it.

However, in order to make your husband aware that housework is not necessarily what you would do with a free hour, you should communicate this whenever possible. As you're vacuuming near him, say things like, "I wish I could sit and read the newspaper once in a while," to which he is likely to respond, "Here, I'm done with the Sports section."

H I M S P E A K

"I'm going to show you how much I value our home."
Translation: I'm going to throw the comforter over the bed every morning and put up a new basketball net.

Second, I now understand that having things clean for my wife is a great way to show love. She really enjoys it when I surprise her and clean something without her asking. When I make bottles of formula or change diapers or make a bed, it's like giving her a dozen roses. You, as the wife of a HIM, need to communicate how much you love him to do some of the little things. Let him think this is his idea or you will spoil it.

Finally, and this has been a slow realization for me, my participation in the cleaning process makes Andrea well up with unparalleled passion. Once, while I was home listening to Andrea interview Dr. Gary Chapman on her radio program, he revealed to a caller that his own wife's love language is acts of service. He said she's much more open to tenderness and romance after he's done a load of dishes or vacuumed a rug.

When Andrea finished the program and returned home, I was

furiously vacuuming the curtains. "I've just cleaned the whole house, done all the dishes, fed and diapered the kids, put them down for naps, and put a soufflé in the oven for dinner."

She forced a smile, handed me a bottle of Windex, and said, "You forgot the windows."

What You Can Do

1. If you can't get your HIM to fall asleep and dream about all the things you do, make a list of each duty and how long each takes you to complete. Show him the list in a nonconfrontational way and see if he begins to understand. Anticipate his turning this into a game called, "I Did More Than You Did Today."

2. Arm wrestle. If you lose, he'll respect you for trying. If you win, threaten to tell his coworkers unless he does the dishes immediately following dinner.

3. Play the helpful game "I took you for granted when . . ." You start by saying something like, "I took you for granted when you fixed the car last year and changed the head gasket on the lawnmower three summers ago. I forgot to tell you I appreciate that." In the best world, your HIM would respond, "Wow, I take you for granted all the time." However, be prepared for him to say something like, "I don't take you for granted. This game is stupid. How do you win? Did you read this in a book? Figures. Where's my paper?"

4. The only sure way to get your HIM to do more around the house is to say, "Honey, I just feel so overwhelmed with all I'm doing around here, and I know it's not fair to ask you to do more than you're already doing, so I'm wondering if we couldn't get someone to come in once a week and help me with all the cleaning." Your HIM will immediately do more than you ever thought he could.

Women are smarter than men because they listen.

PHIL DONAHUE

Women speak because they wish to speak, whereas a man speaks only when driven to speech by something outside himself—like, for instance, he can't find any clean socks.

JEAN KERR

The only time a woman really succeeds in changing a man is when he's a baby.

NATALIE WOOD

Chapter Three

HIMs Communicate Only Under Duress

Remember the filmstrips you used to watch in school when you were a kid? They weren't as good as a movie, but you still got to turn out the lights and watch pictures flipping against the wall. You wanted anything but the reading machine that approached the speed of light. And then there was that awful test afterward. Wait, you're a woman. You probably liked the reading machine and aced the quizzes afterward. You should be ashamed of yourself. You really should. Do you know how much inner turmoil I've gone through because of that reading machine?

Anyway, as I recall it, the teacher picked one lucky person to work the filmstrip projector, while someone else turned on the phonograph or tape player. It was the greatest job in the world. Cecil B. deMille couldn't have had a more important job.

I remember the day my turn came. The light on top of the metal machine made it blistering hot to the touch, and the fan blew in my face. Even though they were small, those projectors weighed about a hundred pounds and sat like tiny brained monsters on the huge rolling carts. I was nervous, of course, wanting to be the best filmstrip operator in the third grade.

The lights went out. The music started. I flipped on the projector light, and the picture said "Start here." I heard the beep and turned to the next frame. Then came another beep and another. And then the beeps started running together and becoming one long beep. People all around were telling me I was on the wrong frame. I flipped forward, then backward, as indecision gripped me. Two frames ahead, one frame back. Did he say "alligator" just now, or were we supposed to be on the ostrich?

"Go back one," a voice whispered.

"Go ahead one," another said.

"Stop fooling with it," the teacher said.

I was in filmstrip limbo. Like when you lean back in a chair and feel it tip backward.

That's how HIMs feel when it comes to communication in relationships. We don't know whether to go to the next frame or to back up three. Was that a beep I just heard from my wife? Am I supposed to be silent and just listen, or jump in and be vulnerable? Should I give her advice?

I am talking to Andrea, if you call it talking. Babbling, actually. Searching desperately for the right thing to say—what I think she wants to hear. I'm trying to appease and please and win her with words. But my mouth has surpassed my mind's ability to process ideas, thoughts, and alibis quickly enough to avoid rendering me a fool. And I'm losing the battle. I would rather be watching a game.

Then she says something that strikes a note with me, that jogs something in my memory. She's talking about the church service and the touching moment when a teenager opened up and shared deep feelings for his parents and how it affected her. That story reminded me that many young people have difficulty with acne, which caused me to think of a guy I knew in high school, who's now an accountant and making at least twice what I'm making, which made me mad and also caused me to think that it's time to send in my quarterly taxes.

H I M S P E A K

"I'm telling you, I'm not angry!!!"
Translation: I'm as mad as I've ever been, but
I'll never admit it.

I'm just about to say, "Hey, you know what? I need to send in those quarterly taxes," and I've just opened my mouth, and she's looking at me with eyes brimming with tears, still thinking about that touching relational moment. My mouth is agape, so I need to say something or she'll think I haven't been concentrating on what she's just said. So I sigh and shake my head and say, "God is good, isn't he?"

I ask myself, *Why am I so afraid to be honest and just tell her that her words made me think of something totally off the subject, and I really don't know what she needs me to say at a moment like that, and most of the time I don't know what she's talking about or how I'm feeling about any subject?* Why am I so scared to tell her that she lost me three paragraphs ago when she started talking about her relationship with a friend and the pain she's feeling? Maybe she'll think I don't love her if I tell her this.

I do love my wife. But I also love caramel corn and baseball, and I get an exhilaration from them that I don't get from a relationship. At least not yet. Caramel corn doesn't care if I helped out in the kitchen yesterday. It simply waits for me in its airtight tub. Crisp and cool. Ever faithful. I love you, caramel corn. You light up my life. You give me hope. To carry on. I have no trouble admitting that I love caramel corn or old songs by Debbie Boone.

And baseball—it never demands anything but undying allegiance. I can give that. All I need is a fresh set of batteries in the remote. (I click between innings.)

But my wife wants a relationship. She wants to be encouraged. She wants me to be vulnerable, and many other things too scary to say out loud or write down. She wants commitment that can't be switched on or plugged in. Interactive human commitment. She wants communication on an intimate level. She wants a relationship she can wade into. I want to splash my feet. It's so much fun to splash your feet on the edge of a relationship. All you have to do is take your socks off.

But deep down I know I want her type of relationship, too. I want to take off more than my emotional socks. Underneath the layers of cheese curls, buttered popcorn, and Pez lies a person of great depth, a person who longs for the same kind of rich, lasting, growing, writhing relationship she desires. But I don't know where that person is, and I'm tired of looking for him. It's easier to pop the top on the caramel corn and turn on another game. *Okay, who took the remote?*

I can fake concern pretty well. I recognize certain tones of voice, certain key words that send my mind into auto-search for compassion. "Oh, that's too bad," I say. "That must really make you feel awful." But these are only jumbled sentences I've heard her say on the phone to her friends. I'm playing my wife back to herself. I'm saying my lines with feeling, but I don't understand them.

This is what it's like inside a HIM's mind. To a HIM, communication means making a grocery list. It's remembering to pick up the kids from the birthday party on time, which means a half-hour either way. HIMs focus on the essentials, the important stuff that has nothing to do with how we feel about anything. Communication to a HIM means standing in the back of church and talking to another HIM. The conversation goes like this:

"How's it goin'?"

"Fine. You?"

"Fine."

"Good."

"How's your car running?"

"Oh, pretty good. I kept hearing this knocking in the engine a couple of weeks ago . . ."

"Really? What was the problem?"

"Well, I took it to the shop, and they finally figured out it was the injector pump."

"Is that so?"

"Only cost $9.95 to fix it."

"Isn't that something. Well I'm glad they were able to fix it."

Now that's a pretty straightforward conversation about an important event in the life of a man. But suppose two women were talking at the same time, only ten feet away, about the same subject. Here's how the conversation would go.

"Hi, Mary, how are you? I've been praying for you."

"Thanks, Kim. (sniff) I really appreciate it."

"Been a hard week?"

"I don't mean to complain, but yes, it's been difficult."

"Do you want to talk about it, or would you just like me to weep with you?"

"I appreciate how much you care. I think I can talk about it."

"Take your time."

"It's the car, Kim. You know that knocking sound I heard a couple of weeks ago?"

"I remember. I prayed about it during my quiet time this morning."

"John finally took it into the shop. I thought it was going to blow up or something, and because it's my car, he wouldn't believe me. You know we have this issue of trust between us, and if he doesn't hear the noise, he thinks I'm just making it up."

"That's too bad. Want a tissue? It's lotion enhanced."

"Thanks for your thoughtfulness. Well, John did drive it to church the other day and heard the same sound. The very next day he took it to the shop, and they found it was some fuel thing that only costs $9.95 to replace."

"Well there's an item for praise!"

"But that's just it! (sniff) Sometimes I feel I'm not even worth the $9.95 it would take to get our relationship to a higher plane."

"Mmmmm."

"Thanks for listening, Kim. I knew I could count on you."

H I M S P E A K

"Tell me what's wrong; I can handle it." Translation: I'm prepared to go out right now and mow the lawn if I can't handle it.

Do you see the difference? The HIMs talked without ever saying each other's names. They probably didn't remember them, but that's beside the point. HIMs don't need names to carry on a deep conversation. We call each other "Bud," "Buddy," "Man," "Hey, man," "Hey, guy," "Hey-y-y-y, look who it is," or any other combination of words that will get us by when we can't think of our friend's name. This is why the inventor of the nametag has to be a man. This is why men wear their names on their pockets at work.

A woman, on the other hand, has a mental list of people's names, and their prayer requests, stitched on the insides of her eyelids. That's why she can always remember a person's name. (I have clinical reports on this, so don't try to deny it.)

"Honey, who's that coming in the door? I know her face, but I can't remember her name," the frustrated man says.

The wife closes her eyes and shakes her head in disbelief as she looks for the name on the back of her eyelids.

"That's your mother, dear," she says.

"Show-off," he says.

Of course, some guys do remember names, but they're always letting everyone know they remember names, which defeats the whole purpose of remembering them in the first place.

"Hi, Bill. Bill, how are you doing? That's a really nice suit, Bill. Can I ask you a question, Bill? How did you get the name Bill, Bill? Are you a William or a just plain Bill, Bill? That's nice, Bill. Good-bye, Bill."

Since he knows the other man's name, he uses it like a salesman to prove he's mastered the art of remembering.

Whether a HIM recognizes it or not, a woman, by nature, is more inclined to care about individuals and their families and to want to communicate about them. It's not that HIMs don't care; we just haven't been conditioned to care.

A young female grows up talking on the phone, learning to discuss "girl" things with her girlfriends, and naturally transitions into a caring, loving, concerned human being.

A young HIM grows up learning to spit. He watches his father spit. He watches baseball players on TV spit. When he's mastered the art of spitting, he learns to hit. He hits the ball, he hits his friends and family members. He jumps. He runs. He bangs into things. He will talk on the phone only as long as he doesn't see anything he wants to hit or spit on. So, he will naturally transition into a grown-up HIM who knows how to hit and spit and run into and over things, but for the life of him he can't remember your best friend's name.

I believe there are also biological reasons why HIMs act this way. I suspect that when a man is about four years old, an explosion inside his brain wipes out half his gray matter, obliterating the part of the brain that remembers names, along with the part that thinks it's okay to ask for directions if you're lost. Fortunately, the sports part of the brain remains intact. The listening part of the brain blows up and is pretty much gone for the rest of his life. This is why he's drawn to explosions; he wants to recapture his other half.

But the biggest part of the brain that survives is the "Why don't you just . . ." lobe. This is the area of the mind that tells your HIM it's okay to solve your problems with a single sentence. It goes something like this.

You have a problem in a valued relationship. Your very best friend, whom you've known since you were two months old, has betrayed you. You can hardly speak through your tears. The one person you've trusted with the details of your life has turned on you, and you're in pain.

Your HIM does not comprehend your emotion. The longest friendship he's maintained is with the mechanic at the garage where he gets the oil changed in his car. He's been going there every three months or three thousand miles for years. He also has no idea that the boy he used to ride bikes with as a kid is now in some cabinet position at the White House. He doesn't connect names from his past.

Furthermore, he can't understand why anyone would even think of telling someone something that the person could use to betray him. Since he doesn't comprehend this, he's quick with an answer.

He looks into your eyes, and with all the sincerity he can muster, says, "Why don't you just drop her and be done with it?"

To a HIM, this is communication. To you, it's reason to get a fireplace poker and chase him around the room. I think I understand these differences pretty well, but I'll admit there have been times when I've used the "Why don't you just . . ." part of my brain with Andrea. The last time I said it she left the room with a strange look on her face. I had no idea she knew where I kept the tire iron, but I haven't used that phrase since.

Your HIM sees you as a project to be fixed. Any communication with you should aid that process. If it doesn't help fix you, it's not important. Listening is not fixing; listening is passively sitting and soaking in another person's life. To a HIM, that does no good. That isn't progress. It doesn't further your life for him to listen.

He doesn't see you as a person with feelings, emotions, and sensitivities. To a HIM, you're a refrigerator with a broken light bulb. You need to be fixed. You need to be changed. You need his logical "Why don't you just . . ." statement to make everything better so you can snap out of your depression and get on with life.

So why don't HIMs communicate?

The answer is, they do. They just do it poorly. This happened to cave men and cave women. The women sat around talking about their problems while the men said "Ugh" and painted pictures on the walls.

At times when Andrea and I are sitting around the cave, she says something about feelings that I truly understand, and I desire to communicate from the depths of my soul. In that split millisecond, I feel an overwhelming sense of love and affection and warmth and tenderness toward her. I want to take her in my arms and hold her like it's my last dying moment, and I have only thirty seconds to express how much I love and care and deeply respect her.

H I M S P E A K

"I want our relationship to be 100 percent open and honest."
Translation: When I say I don't want to talk about it, I mean it.

But indecision and pride keep my arms at my sides. And after about five seconds, I've missed another chance. And it makes me sad, for another two seconds, and then I move on. A HIM always knows how to move on.

But I believe you have reason to hope. If you can understand what a chore communication is for your HIM, you can be of great help. Remember, your HIM will never express your kind of empathy and have the depth of feeling you possess. He won't have as many friends as you to share his life with. You shouldn't try to make your HIM into your own image.

Instead, help your HIM feel comfortable with communication. Begin by listening to his inane sports stories, and ask follow-up questions. What players does he admire most? Did he want to play professionally when he was young?

Gradually move into the areas that are of greater importance to you, remembering that he will want to come back to the sports stories quickly. Your HIM associates intimate communication with pain. If you can show him another side of communication, one that has rewards and is full of joy, he may actually initiate deep communication some day.

If you move toward your HIM in this way, as hard as that may seem, he will likely move toward you. It's a slow and painstaking task, but I've seen it work in my life. In the last few years there have been times when my wife and I talk about things—other than the house, the kids, our work, and the yard—for minutes on end. Mostly we do this during long walks. I opposed this at first, but I've found that walking together drops the defenses and makes the blood flow to that part of a man's brain that opens him to new experiences.

Not long ago, I came home and found the sitter with our kids. I knew my wife was walking, and suddenly I had the urge to communicate great things to her. I actually wanted to talk. I quickly changed my clothes and began walking in the other direction, hoping to meet her somewhere in the middle of her loop. I can't express what a significant change this is in me.

I expected to meet her after about five minutes. I walked for ten minutes and was excited, because I would have even more time with her. I made a mental list of things I would say—encouraging words, thoughts about my feelings toward her. I was going to seize this opportunity for communication.

After about fifteen minutes, there was still no sign of her. I got worried that she might have taken another path. Finally, I saw her in the distance.

I started getting those old feelings men don't like to admit they have. I flashed back to our dating years when I would see her walking in town and my heart would pound faster. My blood pressure would rise, and my throat would get dry. Then I would sense a tingling in my extremities. It was a lot like getting the flu, only without the nausea.

This day, the birds were singing in the trees. The wind whispered in my ear like an old friend, "You're in love. Talk and walk together."

"Thanks, wind," I whispered back. "Have a nice day."

A few paces forward and we were about a block apart. I noticed that her hair was a bit different. She was pregnant now and had gotten a perm, which I thought wasn't worth the money, because perms don't take when you're with child. Still, her figure walking toward me stirred me to thoughts higher than these.

A few steps more and I was smiling. My smile was one of the things that won her heart so many years ago, and I could see her react to it from afar. I tried to decide what vulnerable thing I would share first. But my smile turned downward as I noticed a coat I had never seen her wear before. It was a beauty, but where could she have gotten the money to buy such a coat? Now I was starting to get angry. *You go out and buy a coat and don't tell me? What was wrong with your old coat?*

She smiled nervously, then looked at the ground.

We were only a few yards apart now, my eyes fixed on her, when I realized *this was not my wife!!!* All of those old feelings were coming through for someone I had never even met. Someone at least twenty years older than my wife.

I said hello and briskly walked on. I headed home. I wanted to tell my wife what the other walker had stirred within me. She was there waiting as I burst through the door.

"How was your walk?" I asked.

"Fine. How was yours?"

"Fine," I said.

See how far we've come?

What You Can Do

1. Model good communication to your HIM. Speak in complete sentences. Control your anger. Try not to say "Ugh" or draw pictures on the walls.

2. Affirm your HIM when he does listen and remember things. Give him a treat, but insist that he not pant or wag his tail in excitement.

3. When your husband slips and says, "Why don't you just . . . ," remember that he's a work in progress. Quietly explain to him that he simply needs to listen to you, put his arm around you, and be silent. To quell your temptation to teach him a lesson, keep sharp and heavy blunt objects out of reach.

4. Help take the fear out of communication. If I'm correct about this, deep down your HIM is afraid he's going to say the wrong thing. Begin each conversation with, "You can't say anything that will make me stop loving you." When he feels this acceptance, he will be more likely to communicate on increasingly deeper levels.

5. Tell your husband how good you feel when he asks, "What do you need from me?" Whether it's a point of conflict, an aspect of communication, or a trip to the grocery store, a HIM who asks that question will make great strides with his wife.

Be prepared mentally and physically for intercourse every night this week.

MARABEL MORGAN

Men marry because they are tired; women because they are curious. Both are disappointed.

OSCAR WILDE

I belong to my lover, and his desire is for me.

SONG OF SONGS 7:10

Chapter Four

HIMs Always Think About Sex

*I*f you are a man, and you've picked up this book, stop reading right now. This book is for women only. You would have known that if you hadn't turned directly to this chapter to peek at what I have to say about sex. Shame on you.*

You obviously turned to this chapter first and are now blushing or smiling at being found out. This is a trait of the male in question; he will turn to the part of a book that interests him, no matter how hard the author has worked on the introduction. Okay, man, close the book and go back to the sports section of this bookstore. Or go to the biography section. (HIMs can't stand fiction, because somebody made it up.)

If the Song of Songs in the Old Testament were titled, "Look, Hon—Sex," Christian bookstores would be filled with men looking through different translations and commentaries. From our earliest

---

Shaming does work with HIMs.

pubescent moments, HIMs are curious to see what all the fuss is about.

As a young HIM anticipating marriage, I read Ed Wheat's book *Intended for Pleasure*. With all due respect to Tim and Beverly LaHaye and others who have written eloquently about the marital act, Ed Wheat's book was my choice. Actually, I listened to that book on tape because, like others of my ilk, even books about sex are difficult to read when there are a lot of pages. So I listened to Ed Wheat with my dear bride-to-be, who in all honesty didn't seem nearly excited enough about sex.

I should stop and add a disclaimer for any female reading this book who is engaged to be married. Do not listen to Ed Wheat with your future spouse before the wedding. Listen alone, and talk about what you've heard a couple of weeks later. If you listen to or read Ed Wheat's material together, you will find your fiancé looking at you as if you were an unsliced pot roast in the midst of a pack of hungry buffet patrons. He will ogle and squirm and act like a werewolf at the dusk of a full moon. Beware. This is your last warning.

I was wooing my wife in those days and was willing to go through just about any training or tape series known to man if she would just say yes to my proposal of marriage. So I took Andrea's hand as we sat on her dilapidated couch, in her humble apartment, and listened to Ed Wheat's voice drone through the tinny speakers of a Realistic cassette player. The couch was plaid, the apartment had no air-conditioning, and there were bugs. (I think I may have brought them with me, but that's another story.) She watched the tapes wind on and listened to the voice bleat about the room. At times she would put her hand to her chin and say, "Hmmm," and then go back to thinking about how the bugs got in, or what a lousy couch she had, or any number of things engaged-to-be-married women think about.

But I sat in rapt attention. It takes a lot to make a HIM rapt, unless it's something to do with sex, and I was rapt. The more I listened to old Ed, the rapter I got. Man, was I rapt. I was so rapt I don't believe I could have gotten any rapter.

H I M S P E A K

"So, what do you have planned for today?"
Translation: Let's have sex.

Ed Wheat used big words I had never heard before, and talked about body parts and processes I had heard even less about. And he did it in such a way that someone passing through the room might have thought you were checking on the latest Midwest hog futures. (This, by the way, is not meant in the least to dissuade you from reading and enjoying the work of Ed Wheat, or to demean hog futures.)

But I can still remember the tingly feeling of sitting near the one I loved on that plaid couch, the bugs crawling nearby. Dr. Ed Wheat spoke to us during those hot, sultry nights. I recall the look in my future bride's eyes as we proceeded to turn tape one to the next side. She looked at me, making the passion rise in my soul, and pursed her delicate lips. The light glinted from her hair so that a lovely silhouette appeared against the wall, and she said, with that beautiful alto voice of hers, "Is it me, or is it getting hot in here? I think I'll open a window."

HIMs experience an intense interest in sex that many women seem unable to understand. Women know God put this desire in men's bodies. They understand the physiological processes men undergo, but they still don't "get it."

Let me give you an analogy of how the sex drive affects a HIM. Suppose you were traveling the entire length of the United States in a 1979 Oldsmobile Cutlass Supreme, without air-conditioning, in the middle of July. You are only allowed to stop for refueling. No drinks. You may eat, but only Nabisco Wheat Thins.

You begin in Washington, DC. By the time you get to Pennsylvania, your throat is parched, and the heat is unbearable. When you make it to the Mississippi River, your body is beginning to dry, the very pores of your skin screaming for water.

Through the mountains of Colorado you go, unable to take in the beauty of the Rockies and the rich green valleys, because you're so incredibly thirsty. You throw the Wheat Thins out and are immediately pulled over for littering. You're incredibly thirsty and $500 poorer.

You hit Arizona, and the sun blisters your arms. Your throat feels like sandpaper. California appears, and you recklessly, mindlessly roll on to the Pacific. Just when you think you can go no further, you hit Malibu Beach, and you see the ocean before you, blue and inviting.

You rush from the car, throw off your shoes, and feel the hot sand beneath your feet. You are running, flailing in the wind. And then you see it, a huge cooler filled with sparkling, clear water. You fall to your knees and crawl on your stomach to the dispenser. You pull a white paper cup from above and hold it under the spigot. You reach to push the lever that will start the water streaming from the machine. You place your finger on the side of the lever and push down . . .

There . . . right there; that's how men view sex.

To be honest, I need to change the subject now, because I'm beginning to hear Ed Wheat's voice in my head again.

Many challenges face couples in the area of sex. The first challenge is, of course, children. Sex sometimes leads to children. This truth has hit me six times, so far.

But birthing children isn't nearly as stifling as having them in the house when you feel romantic, which for HIMs is almost all the time. Once I remember following my wife to the shower and peeking in at her as she began to wash her hair. She gasped incredulously.

"What in the world is on your mind?" she asked.

"Well, what do you expect when you parade around here like that?" I replied.

"Parade? Who's parading? I'm taking a shower!"

"Oh, it's so easy for you to wear slinky things around the house all day and then expect it not to do anything to a red-blooded male like me."

"Slinky? What's so slinky about a pair of jeans and a sweater?"

"Well, you should be honored."

Let me be candid for a moment. Andrea and I have found that Saturday mornings are advantageous for romantic forays, particularly when one local Christian radio station plays the program "The Children's Bible Hour." Uncle Charlie and the kids sing and tell stories and teach our offspring many wonderfully spiritual things on Saturday mornings. This allows us to close our door for thirty minutes and enjoy each other.

There's only one problem. Uncle Charlie is aired on other stations, at other times of the day. When I hear the theme for "The Children's Bible Hour," something in my brain says I should close and lock the bedroom door. I find myself strangely drawn to tapes of that program, and play them at odd hours of the day and night, hoping to catch my wife off guard. For us, the "Go along with the story song" has a different meaning. Be careful what you use to occupy your children while you get away. These are the things you will remember for the rest of your life.

There is always the challenge of being interrupted by a crying child, or a child with questions, or a child who has just called 9-1-1 to see if the number really works. One Saturday evening, after we had missed Uncle Charlie in the morning, we all went to bed early. I said something like, "My, my, look at the time. It's five o'clock already; kids, go brush your teeth."

The kids were finally tucked in, and my wife was in bed reading. She held before her a copy of James Fenimore Cooper's *Last of the*

Mohicans. She reads these types of books—works by Dickens, Dostoevsky, Brontë, Chesterton, and other great writers.

I stood in the doorway, brushing my teeth, and suddenly noticed she was laughing. This puzzled me. I have never seen anything remotely comic about the demise of a clan of Native Americans.

"What are you laughing at?" I asked, through a mouthful of Crest.

"Nothing," she said.

The smirk on her face gave her away. She hadn't seen me looking at her and was now caught in the lie.

"What are you laughing about?" I asked again.

HIMSPEAK

"I wonder if there's anything on TV the kids could watch."
Translation: Let's have sex.

She showed me the front of the paperback. On it was a sticker that said $2.99. This is another thing I greatly admire about my wife. She's frugal. This impresses a HIM to no end. Underneath the sticker was a painting of an Indian in full headdress, moccasins, and a little cloth draped in front and back. My wife's face was now red, but I still didn't get it.

"What's so funny about a guy standing by a tree?"

"I was just thinking," she said, "how funny you would look in one of those."

Granted, I gain a few pounds over the winter. It's inevitable for any HIM. The thought of me in that outfit rolled into my mind. I smiled, then pretended to be hurt, which made her laugh again.

I went back to the bathroom and finished brushing my teeth, then pulled a long piece of floss from the dispenser and tied one end to a little bath towel hanging by the sink. Then I pulled the floss tight around my back, tied it to the other end of the tiny towel, and rolled it a couple of times to match the picture on the book. I had no headdress and nothing covering my backside, but I truly felt like Squanto at that moment.

I opened the door and was about to make my grand appearance, when I saw our five-year-old peek around her bedroom door.

"Hi, Shannon," I said. Andrea covered her mouth and turned a deep shade of crimson. I reached to grab a towel.

"Dad," she said, stopping me, "what are you doing?"

I've heard that you tell children only the information they need. So I took a deep breath, grabbed the towel, and backed away. "Shannon," I said, "Mommy and I are playing Indian."

She thought for a moment, then looked back at me. Just before she stuck her two favorite fingers in her mouth, she said, "Oh."

It was enough for her, and enough to make me run for pajamas.

Another challenge couples face surrounds the issue of how many times a week to make love. When you're newly married, both parties seem content to meet somewhere in the middle. This is about four times per week for the female, and seven billion for the male.

In a HIM's mind, being married is like having a free pass to Disneyland. He wants to go to the Magic Kingdom every chance he gets. You are satisfied to visit every few days, or once a week. It makes seeing Mickey and Minnie a new experience each time.

For you, sex is simply one way to intimacy. But for a HIM, sex is the *only* way to achieve intimacy. The HIM smells cotton candy, and sees the brightly colored outfits, and can't stop thinking how great the whole park is. He's just got to get back to the thrill of it all.

You must understand how important sex is to a HIM. Many women are incredulous at the love appetite of their men. This is why most HIMs come home from a trip and race their wives to the bedroom. While a HIM is away, there's only one thing on his mind: He can't go to the Magic Kingdom. He could be on a business trip to Hawaii or fishing in Montana—it doesn't matter. All he thinks about is that he can't be intimate until he gets home. This is why a HIM parks so close to the exit in the airport's parking garage—he wants to get home as quickly as possible.

H I M S P E A K

"Where'd you get that dress?" Translation: That dress really looks beautiful on you. Let's have sex.

I realize that some couples aren't frustrated by the lack of frequency of their sexual relationship. Some men say they're quite happy with an occasional act of intimacy. I am not a psychologist, but I say these guys are in denial. Some women enjoy the physical aspect of marriage more than their husbands. I have serious doubts about those husbands, but I'd be willing to bet they never listened to Ed Wheat.

Because of their heightened desire, few HIMs take responsibility when it comes to birth control, which presents yet another challenge. A HIM believes it is always the woman's job. A HIM will hem and haw about the issue of birth control and will give you a word picture to illustrate his preference for no encumbrances. For instance, he says, "Imagine you were going to Disneyland and you had to wear a laundry bag over your head. You couldn't see Goofy or the fireworks or the majestic buildings. This is how I feel when I'm forced to use birth control."

This is also why your HIM will refuse any kind of surgery to reverse the natural processes of life. Your HIM can hear a pair of scissors snip a mile away, any time you bring up the subject.

"Honey, it's not supposed to hurt at all," the wife says, gently, "and it's outpatient surgery."

"I'm not going to . . . aaaaaaaaaaaaaaahhhhhhhhhhhhhhhh! I don't want to think about it!"

"Oh, don't be such a baby," she says.

"Did you see what they did to me when I was a baby?"

"A lot of men have had a—"

"Don't say it. Don't even say that word! Someone get me an aspirin."

"You know Jim from church, he had a—"

"Don't say it!" he gasps. "Jim is different. And now he'll always be different. Don't you see the finality of all this? Don't you see the anguish and the mental cruelty? This is something you do to dogs and cats, not your husband!"

Your HIM will wait until you're having your next child, and say, "Hey, honey, the doctor says he can take care of that little . . . you know. He says he can just snip a couple of places and you'll be set. Won't feel a thing."

This is said while you're on your back, with feet in stirrups, feeling as if you've just pushed your entire insides through a telephone jack.

Other challenges concern mechanics. Suffice it to say that most men want their spouse to have the agility of a gazelle, the strength of a lion, the spark of a 1965 Mustang convertible, and the breath of a Velamint. These are lofty expectations, but most men I know will settle for the Velamint.

Anger affects the ability to have sex. For women it's difficult to go through an argument of any proportion and begin thinking about intimacy. For men it's exactly the opposite. Having an argument only increases his desire. All the built-up tension and raised voices trip the part of the man's brain that says, "I'm mad, and wouldn't it be great to forget all this and go to Disneyland again?"

H I M S P E A K

"Let's have sex."
Translation: What's for dinner?

To a HIM, sex is escape. Sex after a marital fight means, "I'm sorry I got upset, and I just realized I was a fool, and I'm so glad I married you because you're so good for me. You made me realize how wrong I really am about this, and would you please forgive me?" Sex means never having to say anything like that.

If you want to grow together, you must continually evaluate your view of sex. Does one of you view sex as escape? Does one of you view sex as a chore? Can you both view sex correctly, as a God-given gift? How many times a week should you open the gift?

The only effective way to achieve oneness in this area is to talk about sex. This is one area where communication is no problem for HIMs. However, some women don't like to talk about sex, because they think talking about sex will lead to sex. This is quite true but, speaking for HIMs everywhere, you need to get over that. You really do.

Here's a practical example of one couple's conversation.

HIM: I'm willing to talk about our challenges in this area.

Her: So am I. Let's start with how often we make love.

HIM: See, you make it sound so sterile. It's like we're talking about how often we do laundry.

Her: We don't do laundry. I do laundry.

HIM: Okay, then it's like talking about how often we do the dishes.

Her: We don't do the dishes. I do the dishes.

HIM: Okay, then it's like talking about . . . how about ten times a week?

Her: Two.

HIM: Five.

Her: Three.

HIM: All right, we'll compromise at four.

Her: Deal.

HIM: Now, I want to talk about the way we express our love. Sometimes I think you don't want to talk about what makes it enjoyable.

Her: That's not true. I'll talk about it.

HIM: So what makes it enjoyable?

Her: Uh . . . well, I like it when you massage my neck and then whisper something in my ear. And then when you take care of the kids while I take a bath, that's special.

HIM: Shhh . . .

Her: What is it?

HIM: Did you just hear the Uncle Charlie theme?

Sex is wonderful. Sex is good. Sex is given by God. Sex is intended for mutual pleasure. If you can risk a little and open up about this area of your relationship, it can be an incredible catalyst for communication and intimacy.

What You Can Do

1. Listen to Ed Wheat's tapes together.

2. Read the Song of Songs out loud. Write love poems to each other in response to what you read. Put them to music if you like, and record them so your children will have something to laugh about in a few years.

3. Buy the tape of Uncle Charlie's stories for kids. It's about an hour long. It's really good, especially the one about the boy falling in the lake.

4. Go to your husband's office and ask the receptionist to page "Tiger." Kidnap him and take him on a romantic afternoon get-away. Keep referring to him as "Tiger" throughout the day.

There is no more lovely, friendly, and charming relationship, communion or company, than a good marriage.

MARTIN LUTHER

You can give without loving, but you cannot love without giving.

AMY CARMICHAEL

But men are men; the best sometimes forget.

OTHELLO, WILLIAM SHAKESPEARE

Chapter Five

HIMs Forget Important Days

$\mathcal{I}$f you want to see the most pathetic sight in all of God's creation, go to a greeting card rack on the evening of February 13. There you will see men standing like paralyzed cattle, looking for the right card. It's even more depressing when a HIM shops in a grocery store. I know. I've been there. First, he looks to see how many other men are lined up like love struck lemmings. *Too many*, he thinks, and he heads for frozen foods. Finally, after he's loaded a ton of frozen macaroni and cheese into his cart and things have thinned out, he comes back to the card rack to stop and stare. See his bent shoulders? See the weight of the world upon his back? He reaches for a card, then stops, wondering who's watching. He hears the otherworldly voice of the manager on the loudspeaker, "Bill, cleanup on aisle four. Shoppers, the store is closing in fifteen minutes; please bring your purchases to the registers now. Thank you."

His eyes widen. His pulse quickens. Only fifteen minutes to choose a card for the most important person in the world. He can't try to look good now, the place is closing. He grabs a card. *Too dainty; she'll know the place was closing and I bought the first one I picked up,* he says to himself. The next is too humorous. *She doesn't like to laugh on these kinds of days. She wants me to be serious.*

Next card. Too overtly sexual. *She'll think I only bought the card for one reason. Hmm. Maybe this isn't such a bad card.*

"Shoppers, our store is closing in ten minutes . . ."

Okay, something not too sexual, that isn't dainty or funny, but expresses my love in a down-to-earth way.

Now the scene changes. Our story becomes darker. The doors have been locked, and the squad car pulls up. Stock boys surround your HIM, suggesting possible cards, which he quickly dismisses. "You don't know my wife," he says.

"She'll like anything you get her," the manager pleads.

"You don't know my wife," he says.

"Don't put so much pressure on yourself," a kindly cashier suggests.

The police officer comes in, takes your HIM by the arm, and says, "Okay buddy, it's time to go." Then he pauses. "Hey, is it Valentine's Day tomorrow?"

"Yes," your HIM says on a sob.

"Jumpin' jelly beans, I forgot all about it!"

Then the store manager, who is one of those circumspect shoppers who always gets his wife exactly the right present and buys it a year in advance, gets down on the floor and begins to weep uncontrollably. He is not a HIM. He does not know what we go through. He simply wants to get home to his family.

Believe me, your HIM deserves some compassion when it comes to special days. Whether it's a birthday, an anniversary, Valentine's Day, Christmas, National Truck and Tractor Pull Day, or any other event you view as important, a HIM will almost always forget it, or remember it at the very last moment.

Why does a committed male forget these special times in the life of his wife? Why would a man who is literally prepared to walk over shattered glass to prove his love forget significant days? This man would take toothpicks and erect a monument the size of the Sears Tower in your honor. He would smear liverwurst all over his body and walk into a den of hungry lions to save you or impress you. He would give his life for you. So why does he forget to buy you a present?

H I M S P E A K

"Hey honey, what's the date today?" Translation: Are we near any important dates I've forgotten?

There are two answers. The first is simply *fear*. He is more scared of buying that present than facing the lions. The thought of getting you something that will show he really doesn't know you terrifies him. He's afraid when you suddenly discover he doesn't know you,

you will want to go to counseling. Plus, somewhere deep in his sub-conscious he's saying, "Hey, I'd die for her; what more does she want? A bottle of perfume?"

The second reason your HIM forgets these milestones is *environment*. He may have grown up in a family that didn't take Arbor Day seriously. When I was first married, I could not believe there were so many holidays in the year. Our family celebrated only holidays that featured sporting events, such as Thanksgiving, Christmas, the Super Bowl, and the Fourth of July. (Fireworks is a sporting event.) But Andrea's family must have celebrated all holidays, and even made some up. Grandparents' Day. Columbus Day. Spay or Neuter Your Pet Day. Lincoln's birthday. (They not only celebrated Abraham's but also the birthday of a local friend, Claude Lincoln.)

As I recall, I never had a birthday party with multiple guests outside the family. I believe Andrea rented the nearest civic center. Observing special days was not only a fearful thing, it was a foreign thing to me.

So your HIM forgets. He puts it off. He'll be minding his business, innocently looking at the play-off schedule, and spy the best game of the whole year, then suddenly realize it falls on your anniversary. He realizes this, of course, because you were married on a big play-off day fifteen years before, and he brings this up numerous times to prove his commitment. "I don't watch too much sports! Remember when we were married? Remember the big game that day? Huh? That should count for something! It was called one of the greatest games of the century, and I didn't see one play of that game until the reception."

A HIM would rather have a severe stomach virus than buy a present. Hear HIMs chant, "Down with presents, we want a root canal!" If you want more proof of this, look at the nearest shopping mall on December 24. You'll see nothing but haggard-looking men; some look like deer in the headlights. They trudge from store to store as if they're walking through a ten-foot snowdrift. The pain in their faces, knowing that they don't have a clue what to get their wives, is heart wrenching. You should have pity on these poor creatures, you really should.

During Christmas last year, a department store chain in our town encouraged wives to pin a red dot on their husbands that said, "I'm a guy. I'm shopping. Please help." Wives supplied their husbands with a list of vital statistics: favorite color, dress size, preferred viscosity of motor oil. The department store was inundated by shoppers with red dots. I stayed away from that store. You could feel the dysfunction all the way from the interstate.

I meet fellows every day who say shopping for their wives is the biggest stress of their life. They're afraid they're not going to get the right thing. They're afraid to buy "The Clapper," because now there's "The Smart Clapper" that will turn your lights on and off and leave your TV alone. They're afraid to shop for clothing, because it might be too small and the spouse will think she should lose weight. Or if it's too large, she'll look at him and say, "You think I'm that big?"

Christmas, to a HIM, means failure. These men ask me, "Chris, how do you buy the perfect present? How do you find it so easy to please your wife?" The answer is, I'm just a fellow struggler.

Until now, it's been too painful to discuss what happened a few Christmases ago. However, for the good of HIMs everywhere, and the women who love them, I'm coming out of the closet.

My dear wife. She usually jumps through hoops when I surprise her with a bag of puffed wheat cereal. Really. She's actually done backflips when, without her writing it on the list, I've picked up a box of All Bran. She gets excited over the little things.

You can imagine the response I anticipated when I bought a stereo/CD system for the kitchen at Christmas. Not only did I get the new stereo, I also went to a hardware store and picked out a shelf for it. I stooped so low as to ask for help from the workers, trying to explain where it would go and what screws I would need. I hate that, because the clerks always look at me like I'm supposed to already know. I am not that kind of HIM!

I bought the shelf and the supports, and I kept the stereo a secret from my dear wife and all the children. On Christmas Eve, I set my plan to work. I put a sheet over the doorway to the kitchen and began construction, carefully measuring and drilling. In about forty-five minutes it was complete, and I moved on to the stereo.

There were speaker wires and the antennae but thankfully no screws. I carefully placed the stereo on the shelf, plugged in the headphones, and it sounded fabulous.

I went to bed with great anticipation. I would wake up to hear my wife squeal with delight as she entered the kitchen. She would smother me with kisses and dance about the house with glee. I could hardly sleep I was so excited.

Christmas morning came. She was sitting on the living room couch, waiting with the children, when I came down. I said, "Let me turn on some Christmas music."

Heh, heh, heh, I laughed to myself. *My plan is working to perfection.*

The kids walked into the kitchen, and their mouths dropped open. My wife, my dear wife, walked into the kitchen, looked at the shelf and stereo, crossed her arms, shivered a bit, and said, "Wow, that's nice."

H I M S P E A K

"You just have to understand we're wired differently."
Translation: I forgot your birthday again. Blame my genes.

Nice? I thought. Where were the backflips, the kisses, the dancing with glee? I could have bought a Salad Shooter and gotten that response. This stereo was big bucks, and I had to go outside my comfort zone and construct a shelf. A little part of me died that day. I asked her over and over, "Do you like it?"

"I'll get used to it," she said. "It's just so cluttered in here. When I clean up, I'll be able to enjoy it."

Great. I give her a wonderful present, and she says, "I'll get used to it." The next time she asks me if I love her, I'll say, "I'll get used to you. It's just so cluttered around here. I can't enjoy you right now."

I moped about for a couple of days, then finally got the courage to say, "Why don't you like it?"

"I didn't say I didn't like it."

"You didn't do backflips."

"It's nothing personal. It just looks like it's really expensive, and all I wanted was the old one fixed."

There it was. The cat was out of the bag. She wanted the old one fixed—the one that eats cassette tapes like a hungry teenager. She wanted that more than a new one.

I tried to explain that fixing the old one would probably cost as much as buying the new one, but she quizzed me on the word *probably*, and I failed.

"I'll take it back," I said.

"You don't have to take it back; I'll get used to it."

I felt like a dog who had just lost a bag full of milk bones. I hung my head and said, "Do you like the shelf?"

"I love the shelf," she said.

I boxed up the stereo and took it back to the store. "Is there something wrong with it?" the man asked, looking over the box.

"It's a long story."

"You don't have to explain it, son," he said with great understanding, as if he'd seen this many times before. "We'll credit your Visa."

After talking with Andrea, I learned that she looked at the gift as another machine in a house full of broken machines. Since I insist on keeping everything, her first thought was where we would store the old one, instead of how much time, effort, and money I had put into buying the new one. She learned that I must be allowed to be disappointed. We finally worked it through.

The day after I took the stereo back, she was cleaning the kitchen. She stood up and banged her head on the shelf. She put her hand on my arm.

"I really love the shelf," she said. "Maybe it could be just a little bit higher."

HIMs do take the issue of buying gifts seriously. They want to please. That's why I've included the following material to help you educate your HIM about how to buy you presents. I've come up with some surefire, can't-miss ways to help a HIM buy the perfect present *every* time.

Understand that these tips are adaptable to your specific situation and the chemistry of your particular marriage. These tips will vary with the number of children you have, the number of years you've been married, the level of anger in your marriage, and the number of times your HIM has said, "I really meant to get you something, but I forgot."

HOW TO HELP A HIM BUY THE PERFECT PRESENT EVERY TIME
Ten Tips for Stress-Free Shopping

Tip #1: "Mind over Present"

No matter how clueless your HIM is, he must give the impression that he knows exactly what he's doing. The worst thing he can ask is, "Hey, honey, what do you want for Christmas?" He must understand that this is like waving a red flag in front of a charging bull. He must shop with confidence. He should move around you with an air of knowledge—that suave, debonair approach—that says, "I know you and I know me, and I know how much is in my account. I have you figured out, baby." Remember to impress upon him that it's not what he buys, but how confident he is while selecting it.

Tip #2: Listen

Encourage your HIM to listen when you talk on the phone, when you talk to the kids, when you talk to yourself (if you do that). If you talk in your sleep, have him record the conversation. Have him ask leading questions. Again, he should not ask, "What do you want for Christmas?" I can't stress this enough. I know men who have no kneecaps because they didn't heed this tip.

He must ask questions such as, "If you were on a desert island and could only bring one thing from your favorite catalog, what would it be?" Then, and this is the tricky part most men get tripped up on, he must listen. That's right, listen. Have him take notes if he has to.

Tip #3: Watch

Open a catalog and linger over the things you love. If you're walking through the mall, looking for things for the kids, stop in front of a window as if you were Tiny Tim gazing at the toy train. He must watch you in the same way he analyzes the weaknesses in his favorite football team's defense. He may want to videotape you for instant replay.

Tip #4: Knowledge Yields Victory

This is a given, but it bears repeating. If a HIM can become a student of his wife, if he watches and listens, he will know her. He'll know what kind of dressing to order for her salad. Does he think it's Lemon Dijon or French? He needs to know this.

When he does remember the little things, giggle with delight. A HIM cannot resist a delighted giggle when he remembers your shoe size or how much cream to put in your coffee. He should know that you don't like to open the closet and have him jump out in a ski mask, baying like a wolf. (I've found that my wife just plain hates that type of thing, but I do it occasionally anyway.) However, if he buys the right present, it won't matter.

Tip #5: The Shotgun Approach

I do not mean he should buy you a gun. Unless, of course, you really want one, and then I suggest a Remington 12-gauge and a box of Pink Lady shells.

By the shotgun approach I mean volume, volume, volume.

Encourage him not to worry about one big gift. Instead, suggest he give candles, tickets to a concert, a scarf, a new dictionary, flowers, perfume, a subscription to your favorite magazine, a book, a gift certificate to a Christian bookstore, one of my other books, a gift certificate for a Saturday off from all duties with the kids, and a box of chocolates.

HIMSPEAK

"Did you just see that creative advertisement on TV?"
Translation: I'm getting you a Chia Pet for our anniversary.

This year for Valentine's Day, I put up signs everywhere, a week before, that said, "It's coming. Right here! Don't Miss It!" Then, each morning when Andrea woke up, there was a different present waiting for her as we counted down the days. This not only made her feel valued, cherished, and special, it also made her think of what she could do for me in return, which is a great motivator for a HIM. Reward.

Remember, tell him not to buy a gun, but to overwhelm you with his vast wealth of creativity. I believe he will thank me on Valentine's evening.

Tip #6: Ask a Friend

Have your husband ask your best friend what you would like. (And if you're like my wife, you have about seventy-five really close friends.) This not only gives him a good idea, it will thrill him to hear the conversation after you've opened your present.

"Wasn't that sweet of your husband?" your friend will say.

"What do you mean?"

"Didn't he tell you? Oh, he's just so darling. He called me and asked what I thought you would want for Christmas. Wasn't that sweet? I think it took a lot of guts for him to do that."

"Yes, I guess it did."

"What did he wind up getting you, the perfume?"

"No."

"He didn't get the indoor spa, did he?"

"No."

"Did he give you the manicure, pedicure, massage package?"

"No."

"Well what did he get you?"

"A 12-gauge semiautomatic and some bird shot."

"Oh."

Tip #7: The Gift of Time

They say it's the most precious commodity these days, and it's really cheap. Tell him how special an overnight getaway would be. Leave paper lying around that is appropriate for coupon creation. Imply that arranging the baby-sitting details gets major points.

Or suggest that he give you the gift of time away by yourself. "I would love to have a Saturday afternoon to myself to just shop, read, or be alone and think of how much I love you."

This scores points with you and lets him enjoy the football game and order pizza so the kids think he's a prince.

Tip #8: Behind the Back

Have your kids run interference. Give them a little extra allowance, or tell them this is part of their dramatic training. Have them go to your HIM and say, "Boy, Dad, I really feel sorry for Mom."

"Why is that, Son?"

"She feels really bad that you won't know what to get her for Christmas. It's really sad."

"Well, do you know what she wants?"

See? You'll achieve a great victory here if only your HIM will pay attention to his kids.

Tip #9: The Phone

Pretend you're one of those sweepstakes announcers with the really wacky voices. Call him on the phone and say this:

"Hi there, Mr. Wilson. Did you know you're a winner?"

"Oh yeah?"

"Yes, and you've just won a free consultation on what present to buy your wife!"

"Really?"

"That's right, and we've already done the sizing and measuring. All you have to do is go down to the store and pick it up!!"

"Wow!"

Tip #10: Creative Questions

About a week before Christmas (or any other big day) ask if you can guess what present he's chosen.

"Well, I don't know . . ." he stammers.

"Oh come on, let me guess."

"Okay."

"Is it a gift certificate?"

"Ha! I'm not telling. Guess again."

"Well, is it that book I told you about last week?"

"What book was that?"

"You know, the new one about making your relationship stronger, by that marriage counselor?"

"What's his name?"

"Gary Smalley."

"Ha ha ha, I'm not telling. Guess again."

HIMSPEAK

"You just wait until next Valentine's Day. It's gonna be a doozie."
Translation: I'm actually thinking about buying something other than a card next year.

You might get three or four really great presents if he listens closely.

Of course, you could always take matters into your own hands.

You could buy and wrap your present, put it under the tree, and pretend he bought it for you. This is way too easy and takes the enjoyment out of the special day. Simply reassure your HIM with the tips listed above, and make him think he's a winner in this area, even if he does get you a garage-door opener.

What You Can Do

1. Photocopy the ten tips for HIMs and give them to him. Chances are he's going to lose the list the first few times, but give it to him anyway.

2. Encourage your HIM to think positively about gifts, and give him verbal affirmation. Tell him it's very important for him not to say the following when handing you your gift: "No matter how hard I try, I know it's never going to be enough." Suggest another sentence he can say, such as, "I've tried really hard to show you how much I love you with this gift, but as good as it is, it still won't capture all the feelings I have for you."

3. What gift have you received that really made you feel loved and cherished? Do you need one in a different color?

4. Okay, so you've never received a gift that made you feel loved and cherished. I know. But haven't you ever gotten something that at least made you feel warm inside? (Not counting the toaster.) Tell your HIM about that experience.

5. Engaged readers, never have a June wedding. I suggest you get married near a national holiday such as the Fourth of July or Elvis's birthday. This way your HIM will associate the anniversary with something he'll remember. For example, Andrea and I were married on December 18, one week before Christmas. Every year I know my anniversary is exactly seven days before the biggest holiday of them all. (In case you want to send a present, because of the size of our family, we're now registered at your nearest Piggly Wiggly.)

Men live by forgetting——women live on memories.

T. S. Eliot

Men have sight; women insight.

Victor Hugo

Whoever wants to know the heart and mind of America had better learn baseball.

Jacques Barzun

Chapter Six

HIMs Keep Their Feelings in a Closet

I have never been comfortable with my wife crying in public. I recall once driving up to our apartment building and sitting in the parking lot so she could stop crying before we got out of the car. When I divulged this information in a counseling session, the counselor just stared at me.

"Why did you do that?" she asked. "What were you afraid of?"

"I don't know; I just don't like her to cry in public. They might think I'm beating her or something."

"Do you beat her?" she asked.

"No," I said with a laugh.

"Then why are you so concerned about what other people think?"

I thought about that question for five years and still couldn't come up with a satisfactory response. Then I heard Dr. Sandra Wilson, a psychologist who talks about men as emotional lepers, and I realized that was it. That was my problem. I'm an emotional leper.

The physical disease of leprosy deadens the nerves at the surface, and the victim often sustains injury, because pain is not detected. Emotional leprosy is similar. If your HIM stays distant, has very few friends, discloses nothing, feels little empathy, and generally has no idea what the word *feeling* means, he is an emotional leper. When something tragic happens, he displays the wrong emotions. He'll laugh when he's supposed to cry. When a conversation becomes emotional, he clears his throat, changes positions in his chair, and begins to suck air between his teeth. He makes jokes during serious events and generally drives you crazy doing so. Dr. Wilson believes the church and society not only condone but also encourage men toward leprous living.

HIMs have great difficulty accepting the fact that they have emotions. Though HIMs are red-faced and filled with anger, they will rarely admit what they're feeling.

"Boy, you're really angry about that, aren't you?" you say in the midst of a verbal brawl with your HIM.

"I am not angry!" he shouts.

"You're not angry?"

"No!!!!!!!!!"

"When a person turns red, yells a lot, and points his finger at someone, I usually associate that behavior with anger."

"Well, I'm not angry," he says, turning purple. "And don't tell me how I'm feeling. If there's anything that gets to me, it's people who try to convince me they know how I'm feeling."

"Oh, so I'm really getting to you?"

"No! Nobody's getting to me. I'm fine."

Anger is the main emotion one thinks of when discussing the HIM. Actually there's a full range of emotions down there, but they're so tightly bound that anger is the only one that surfaces. And a HIM will never admit this until someone is standing over him with a cell phone, dialing 9-1-1.

You see, HIMs don't know what they feel. For a HIM, trying to figure out feelings is like someone from another country trying to figure out football.

"Why do they run after each other?"

"Because they're all trying to get the ball."

"Can't they afford more than one ball?"

"They can, but that's the whole point of the game. You try to take your ball to the opponents' end zone and score."

"So if you get the ball to the other side, you win?"

"Yes."

"Then why don't they just give it away in the middle and nobody will get hurt."

"You don't understand."

Now, take this same inability of a HIM to understand what he's feeling into his everyday life. To this day, when someone asks me, "How's it goin'?" I have no earthly idea what answer to give. I have not considered how it's "goin'" for most of my adult life, because I've lived under the assumption that it really doesn't matter how it's "goin'" because it wouldn't change anything if I did know. Some HIMs label this as being humble—not focusing on self. Actually,

non-self-awareness is the opposite of humility. It's a hedonistic practice that keeps a HIM mired in the manure of self without recogniz-
ing the stench. (Sorry. I got a little carried away there.)

"I don't know how I feel about that."
Translation: I haven't had a conscious feeling
about anything in the last thirteen years.

When someone asks me, "How's work going?" I think, *Well, I'm
still employed, and my HMO keeps my kids relatively healthy, and I haven't
signed up for the pension plan like I should have about ten years ago . . .*
What in the world do people mean when they ask questions like that?
I have no idea. Do you want to know how my relationship is going
with my boss, or whether the people I work with like me? Is that the
question? If it is, I'm not answering, because I don't know. Unless
there's something cataclysmic happening, I have no idea how it's goin'!

On the other hand, if you ask my wife, "How's it goin'?" she will
take you through all the aspects of our family, her spiritual life, and
everything from her inner struggles to the timeliness of the mail delivery. And she'll do this in less than fifteen seconds if she has to. She
can fit all of life into the rubric of "How's it goin'?" This skill is dou-
bly frustrating for the HIM. Not only is he out of touch with his emotions, he sees a person before him who understands her life and can
easily communicate it. This, of course, leads to many jokes about

"those silly, emotional women." This derision stems from envy, but a true HIM would deny that.

You see, from infancy a HIM is taught that emotion equals weakness. Becoming emotionally involved in an issue causes one to lose objectivity and begin "feeling" for a moment, and feeling anything is bad when you're trying to make a decision. You should use your head, not your heart, according to a HIM.

Studies show that male infants are just as emotionally expressive as females, but at a very early age they are taught to suppress feelings and "act like a big boy." HIMs are encouraged to stifle emotions such as sadness and fear, while girls don't seem to suffer such constraints. Psychologist Ronald Levant of Harvard Medical School says that by the time they reach adulthood, "Men are usually able to keep their emotions in a closet. And when you do that, you begin to lose the ability to feel."[1] (Don't bother asking a HIM what he thinks about those statistics.)

Levant goes on to say that men feel close to other men by doing things rather than by talking. When a woman comes to the end of a visit with a close friend, she'll give her friend a firm hug and say, "I just appreciate your friendship; thanks for being here." They may just stand there and hug, exhaling, and then part, one standing at the door while the other walks away. A tear may cascade down the woman's cheek as she watches her dear friend approach her home across the street and pause at the door, giving one final wave before she goes inside. Friends make life worth living.

A man would never do such a thing with his friend, because they've just spent the last three hours installing a water heater. Can you imagine the conversation before one HIM heads home?

"I'm so glad we were able to spend this time together, Joe. It really means a lot."

"Don't think anything of it, Claude. I would install this water heater just for the pleasure of your company."

"Well (sniff), that's just the beautiful thing about you. You put people ahead of tasks every time."

"Go ahead and let it out, buddy."

"Oh, you're so understanding."

"Thanks. See you at my house next week when we put in our new deck."

"I'll be counting the days."

Do you think any self-respecting man would say such a thing? Who needs a hug when you've been sweating pipe the whole day? That's closeness. Friends don't make life worth living, they make jobs around the house much easier.

Many HIMs associate feelings with nothing but negative emotions. Perhaps their fathers abandoned the family, or their moms were alcoholics. Maybe the family was shunned by friends. A HIM may recall a particularly tumultuous dating relationship where the girl rejected him and caused great anguish. *Emotion can cause you,* the HIM thinks, *to become infatuated with another person and want to be with that person all the time and hold hands and buy flowers and spend money on a whim. Then the girl may dump you.* This is why your HIM expels great amounts of air when you say, "Remember when we used to hold hands and walk along the river when we first met?"

"Whew, I'm glad we don't have to do that anymore," he says. And he really means it. Your HIM remembers the incredible amount of emotional energy he expended and the fact that if you had said no when he proposed, he would be floating in that river right now. He remembers the flutter of his heart when he saw you across a crowded room, the perfume you wore, and he thinks marriage is much easier, because he shouldn't have to work at it so hard. He doesn't have to feel anything anymore. He just had to say, "I do," in front of a large number of people, and that did it.

H I M S P E A K

"I cry all the time; you just don't see it." Translation: When I feel like crying, I hide.

Emotions force HIMs to go beneath the surface. Emotions push a man to break the crusty ground on top and dig deep inside. Emotion brings pain. Emotion tightens the chest and raises blood pressure. Emotion can't be controlled, and HIMs hate anything they can't control. It's just easier on a HIM if he gradually pushes those feelings into his closet and puts on the emotional leper suit.

Let me give an example of what goes on inside the mind of a HIM when trying to deal with an emotion. Suppose you are sitting down at the end of a long evening, the children are in bed, and you are upset about the fact that your HIM has not done enough around the house. This is a constant, universal issue of HIMdom. He doesn't do the dishes or the floors or whatever it is you think he should do, and you feel alone.

"I want to bring something up with you, and I just don't know how to do it," you say.

She's leaving me, he thinks. *I'm starting to feel all tight in the chest.*

"So, what is it?" he asks, putting down his power tool catalog.

"Well, I don't know how to say this so you won't get angry . . ."

She's canceled the cable.

"I won't get angry. Just tell me what it is," he says, his teeth clenched ever so slightly.

"It's just that you don't react well when I bring these things up . . ."

She wants me to do more around the house. "Would you just say it already?!? Good grief, I hate these conversations when you go on and on about how angry I'm going to get and how I don't react well to things, and then you tell me you want me to put a new washer on the kitchen faucet!"

"How did you know?"

"Know what?"

"That the kitchen faucet needs a new washer?"

At this, the HIM immediately leaves the house for the hardware store, pushes the employees around, then comes back to install the washer. This is why hardware store workers should buy lots of insurance. They encounter angry HIMs whose wives have just asked them to get more involved around the house. This phenomenon of going to the store happens with things as small as faucets and as big as air-conditioning units. HIMs would rather, when confronted on an emotional level, go out and buy thousands of dollars worth of equipment than deal with the emotions they feel when they're confronted with anything. HIMs don't want to feel shame. They don't want to feel anger. They will immediately buy something and install it just to get rid of the feeling.

A HIM will also get up and leave if the conversation gets too intense. When he reaches the boiling point, or the point at which he knows he's wrong and there's nothing he can say to convince you he's not, he gets up and leaves.

"I wish you wouldn't get up and leave," you say.

"I have to exercise right now."

"Why right now? Why can't we talk this through?"

"I'm retaining water."

"That makes no sense."

"Look, if I stay here, I'm just going to get upset and yell, and I don't want to do that, so I'm going in the other room."

My theory is that we HIMs get our emotions out during sporting events. If you sit close to your HIM's recliner with a bowl of popcorn, during a play-off game, you'll see what I mean. At some point your HIM will be so angry or elated that he will jump up and knock the bowl right out of your hands. If his children did such a thing, he would skin them alive. Since it's him, he will either roll his eyes or blame you for sitting too close. The point is, he's expressive, he's boisterous, he feels free to be himself only in this situation. The rest of his life is controlled. Rational. Ordered. But when it comes to sports, he's a little child who hasn't learned it's not HIMly to express emotion.

If you really want to understand the heart and mind of a HIM, learn what he loves. For me, it's baseball. I am still exhilarated by the sights and sounds of a ballpark. The lush green grass. The bright white lines. The "crack" of a wooden bat, and the "thump" of a ball hitting leather.

I remember summer nights when my father and I pitched to each other in the twilight, the crickets as our audience. In my family, baseball was the conduit to feeling. It freed us to cheer with abandon. We groaned and mumbled at managerial ineptitude and really felt the sting of losses. But we felt. We experienced. Your HIM's emotional connection could be football or chess or ice fishing or bowling, or a million other things.

HIMs do life on a diamond or a gridiron, between imaginary boundary lines. Our minds hold fences and goalposts that seem legitimate boundaries for our emotions. We find ways of expressing ourselves that are safe to us. Look at any play-off game in a frigid climate and you'll see grown men without shirts, their bodies painted the home team's color.

Announcer 1: Look at those guys down there without shirts on.

Announcer 2: It must be five below zero down there.

Announcer 1: Yeah, and they're having the time of their lives.

Announcer 2: They're crazy, that's what they are.

Announcer 1: Let's see if we can hear what they're saying. Can we get a camera close enough to hear what they're saying?

Natural Sound: Wooooooo Wooooooo!!! Go-o-o-o-o-o!! Wooooooo, go-o-o-o-o-o-o-o-o!

Announcer 1: This is what it's all about.

Announcer 2: I still think they're crazy.

When you see a HIM at the deathbed of another HIM, bending near for possibly the last few words that will pass between them on earth, they cling to the latest score or bring up the no-hitter they experienced together. This round leather ball and the game that goes with it is all that many HIMs have to express their emotions and tie them to others. It's a fleeting bond. It's the back and forth tossing of a ball, without words. It's the catch, the embrace, the throw. Catch, embrace, throw. It's all many of us have to call our own. This is why films such as *Field of Dreams* have such a hold on us. Our fathers are in the cornfield, our emotions are in the closet.

This is the reason so many retiring athletes lose it on the day they announce they're leaving the game. The athlete stands at a podium with his wife by his side and looks out on the sea of media faces and cameras. He speaks in squeaks and squawks, and the tears flow. I'm convinced that something inside the man clicks at that very moment. He sees his father, throwing that ball time after time; all the Little League games; all the snow cones his mother bought; all the trophies and practices and effort that went into this moment. For the first time, he feels something other than the thrill of victory and the agony of defeat. He feels the bittersweet tug of relationships—the players he's leaving behind, the pranks they pulled in the locker room, which he will no longer be involved in, and the fact that he will, from now on, always be a spectator and not a participant.

HIMSPEAK

> "I don't know why you always have to be so emotional."
> Translation: I have no idea what to do when you cry.

What can you do about your HIM's emotional leprosy? Perhaps you first need to grieve about your HIM. It's a sad thing to see someone who can't deal with life on an emotional level. Grieve his decision to enter into only part of living. But be careful that you don't wind up carrying the entire emotional load in the family. I see many HIMs who are stoic, go-with-the-flow types who let their wives become emotional wrecks simply because they refuse to get involved in important aspects of the family. I am not suggesting you should grieve in the place of your HIM, but realize that he's not all he could be. Your job will be difficult to keep in balance, but more rewarding when he finally comes around.

Second, resist the urge to make your HIM feel something. There have been times over the past few years when Andrea would purposely goad me into feeling. She wanted to see something—any kind of emotion—even if it was anger. She wanted to know that I care.

Someone has said that the opposite of love is not hate but indifference. This is why she tries so hard to get me to express things, but it sure makes no sense to a HIM like me.

While writing this book, Andrea told me our seventh child was on the way. When the EMTs finally revived me, I was very excited. Then one morning, Andrea began having difficulties with the pregnancy. I had the day off and was prepared to stay in my office the whole day and get lots of work done. I was in my own little HIM world. When a friend encouraged her to stay in bed the whole day, I grudgingly offered to care for the kids. I really didn't know what to do or how to handle this crisis moment. I made a few HIM-like remarks, such as, "It's going to be okay," or "If things don't turn out, we can still have fun trying for another." I still remember the look on her face as she stared at me from the couch.

"Don't you feel anything?" she asked.

"Of course I feel something," I said, trying to figure out if I felt anything. "I just don't feel it the same way as you. What is it you want?"

This, by the way, is the ultimate HIM question. We want to know what you want, so we can do it and fulfill our obligation as quickly as possible.

"I just want you to love me," she said.

"But I do love you. I've taken care of the kids all day and brought you oatmeal and fixed lunch, and I even went to the store! Plus, we don't even know what's going to happen. It may turn out fine. What more do I have to do?"

"Why don't you just sit by me and tell me you don't understand but you want to? Why don't you just tell me you love me and that you'll be here?"

Those sentences, as hard as they were for me to hear and for Andrea to divulge, were worth gold. When the doctor confirmed her worst fears, and she lost the baby, I picked out a card I felt appropriate, then bought a gift in memory of our baby. I was able to move toward her in a way that communicated my emotion and devotion for her that was safe for me but still pleasing to her. If she had expected me to read her mind, she would still be grieving my uncaring attitude. She took the time and emotional energy to teach me, and it made a big difference.

Take every opportunity to model a healthy emotional existence for your HIM. Don't hide your tears, even if it makes him uncomfortable. Don't allow his lack of emotion or overabundance of anger to keep you from expressing yourself. It becomes easier for your HIM to change when he sees your emotions in the context of day-to-day living.

I've found that my wife responds well to the question, "What do you need from me right now?" She doesn't like, "What do you want me to do?" It feels too obligatory. But, "What do you need?" can encompass so many things a HIM won't understand, such as just listening to you or just holding you. When he has no idea what to think or do or how to react, encourage your HIM to ask you, "What do you need from me?"

Studies suggest that men are getting smarter in this area. Many men I know feel freer now to talk about some deep issues. Some men are opening up and talking about their feelings, and these men aren't engaged to be married or even dating someone! Some of these men have been known to be married as many as ten years, or even longer!!!

To get a HIM used to dealing with his emotions, you must give him the space and time to grow. And you must be prepared when this overstuffed closet of emotions opens and spills out on you. That experience can be quite scary. Be prepared to fight the inclination to say, "Go back to being a leper!" One of the great fears of a HIM is that when he finally gets up the nerve to self-disclose, he will not be accepted. He fears that his feelings will be treated as foolish. If he finally gets rid of some emotional baggage and tells you what's really going on inside him, you might be appalled and not want him around anymore. So decide whether you really want to know the truth before you beg him to share his life. You must be committed, no matter what comes out of him, to deal with the effects of a bursting dam. Having said this, if you choose to accept this mission, you can be an incredible agent of change in the life of your HIM. It may seem like an impossible mission at this point. But don't give up.

And if he never changes, look at the bright side. He can't complain that you hurt his feelings if he doesn't have any.

1. Marilyn Elias, "Men make strides in closing emotional gaps," *USA Today*, 26 August 1991, section D.

What You Can Do

1. Encourage your HIM to keep an "Emotional Journal." Be prepared to stumble upon it one day and read the following: "Today I sensed a deep feeling. I did not shrink from it but owned that deep feeling. I think it was anger, but I'm not sure. It could have been shame. Then again, it could have been fear. But I'm afraid to think it could be fear, and I'm ashamed of that, so I think I'll stick with anger. Yes, I'm angry. I think I'll turn on a game now."

2. To help him get a handle on his emotions, list several emotions a person might feel and tape the words to various pieces of fruit. For example, the apple of anger, the kumquat of fear, the pineapple of guilt. Have him pick up each piece of fruit and describe a time when he felt angry, fearful, or guilty. Validate his feelings. Then make fruit salad.

3. Here is a list of things that may move your HIM to emote. Read these aloud to him, and see if you get a response.
   - a child's cry
   - a favorite toy he remembers
   - the first book his mother read to him
   - the gentle breathing of sleeping children
   - the first picture he kept of you
   - a wet basement
   - a bases-loaded walk
   - the "no touchback" rule
   - Little Debbie (or any other favorite snack cake)

- his first kiss

- his first car

- his first job

- the feeling he gets when a child falls asleep on his chest

4. Draw boundaries for unacceptable expressions of emotion and be willing to let him do the same. For example, it is unacceptable for him to express his anger at you by yelling at the children. Likewise, it is unacceptable for you to express your anger by slamming the silverware drawers or preparing Alpo fettuccine for dinner.

Just because you're miserable doesn't mean you can't enjoy your life.

ANNETTE GOODHEART

Nothing so stirs a man's conscience or excites his curiosity as a woman's silence.

THOMAS HARDY

Plans fail for lack of counsel, but with many advisers they succeed.

PROVERBS 15:22

Chapter Seven

HIMs Won't Go to Counseling

"Will you go to counseling with me?"

Ladies, these words fill a HIM with sheer dread, like getting a draft notice to an unpopular war. If you ever go for help, and the counselor asks you to bring your husband, don't ask your HIM, "Will you go to counseling with me?" He will not.

You see, your HIM looks at marriage differently than you. He does not look for a growing, deepening relationship. He wants a companion who will talk with him when he needs conversation (every few weeks), do his laundry when he needs clothes (every few days), and have sex with him when he needs intimacy (every few hours). But your HIM does not look at the marriage as something that needs work. The yard needs work, not the marriage.

In Leo Tolstoy's *Anna Karenina*, the character of Levin represents a HIM. I have not read *Anna Karenina*, but my wife has, and she showed me this wonderful passage.

He was happy; but, having embarked on married life, he saw at every step that it was not at all what he had anticipated. At every turn he felt like a man who, after admiring the smooth, happy motion of a boat on a lake, suddenly finds himself in it. It was not enough to sit still without rocking the boat—he had to be on the look-out and never forget the course he was taking, or that there was water beneath and all around. He must row, although his unaccustomed hands were made sore. It was one thing to look on and another to do the work, and doing it, though very delightful, was very difficult.[1]

This is your HIM. He wants all the joy of being on the water without having to work to get there. So if you want your husband to expend enough energy in the relationship to go to counseling, you are going to have to do what Andrea did.

Several years ago she was going through a very deep valley. It happened just after our first child was born—the moment when many wives realize they've made a big mistake, because now they have to parent two children. I was tempted to point out that hormones play a part in these difficult days; then I realized I should never point to hormones, and I backtracked. But deep down I knew she had to resolve bigger issues than estrogen.

She was struggling with her place in the world as a woman—as a mother, a daughter, a wife. She struggled with the fact that I laid around the house all weekend, watched too much television, and only held the baby when it was "convenient." Of course, I thought I was being the perfect husband for taking the baby for a stroll every few days or holding her on my lap while I watched a game (or four). My wife did not. She had goals and dreams for our marriage. I had not even thought about goals for our marriage. I believed that saying "I do" was enough, as long as I kept saying "I do."

Andrea started having trouble sleeping, and someone suggested she keep a journal. One day I walked by the journal, lying on the couch, and read something like the following: "Why do I hate him, Lord? Why can't I love him like I want to? I want to love him. Help me love him. Why can't I love him? I hate him, and I feel so bad about it. WHY CAN'T I LOVE HIM???"

The pencil must have broken at this point, because the next words were in very angular print that read, "Because he lays around all weekend and won't *do* anything!"

So much for waiting for the still, small voice.

I lovingly sat down with her, and we talked, which means I talked, and she tried to talk and then started crying, and then I went into the other room. When I had the guts to return, she told me she wanted to see a counselor.

"My friends think it will help," she said.

"I know you better than they do," I said. "What do they know?"

I recoiled at the idea of counseling. First, I balked at the time commitment. I would have to take two hours out of the middle of my day to watch our child. Second, (actually this was first, but I lied), I complained about the money. How much was it going to cost, especially if I couldn't watch our child and we had to get a baby-sitter? She answered by saying, "Well, how much is our marriage worth?" My answer to that, though I kept my mouth shut, was that our marriage would be worth a lot more if we didn't have to pay someone for counseling. Third, I said that counseling wouldn't help. She'd go a couple of weeks and see that things weren't really that bad. Compared with other marriages, ours was in the top percentile. Or, perhaps the counselor would go so slow that Andrea would have to keep coming back week after week, then move to twice a week.

HIMSPEAK

"I don't believe in all that psychobabble stuff." Translation: I don't want to go to counseling.

But the real reason I didn't want her in counseling was something entirely different. In the mind of a HIM, the mere suggestion of going to a counselor means *failure*. He takes it personally. He thinks he hasn't lived up to his end of the marriage bargain, which wasn't much of a bargain from his wife's perspective. He hasn't loved her enough or said "I do" enough or been strong enough to help her overcome whatever demons hound her. He feels that it's his fault she has problems. So if he can keep her from going to a counselor, he can keep up the illusion that everything is okay. I know it sounds strange, but it's true.

I finally convinced my wife that counseling was not necessary. I had the answers to her problems, and they were *her* problems. Her issues. She was the one who needed to be fixed. Then I tried to fix her.

Twenty minutes later, bruised, confused, and with all my emotional juice drained, I gave up and told her she ought to go see a counselor. All the things she brought up were true, especially the parts that had to do with me, but I couldn't face them. I remember turning my head, waving at her, and saying, "I don't care how long it takes. I don't care how much it costs. Just go and get fixed, and be the woman God wants you to be." It usually only takes about twenty minutes of weeping to convince a HIM that a woman needs professional help, because he just can't stand the tears.

I figured counseling would take a couple of weeks. It took a lot longer. These people go to school for a long time to learn all about the human condition, right? They ought to be able to diagnose the problem quickly. My mechanic never went to grad school, and he can tell me what's wrong with my car just by listening to it idle.

Well, it took longer than a month. It took a lot longer. Even with the counseling fee adjusted to our income it was taking way too long. "Doesn't that counselor take coupons?" I asked. "Maybe you could go every other week and cry twice as hard."

It was difficult to let her go. I would walk around Sears thinking, *I wonder if everyone here in the automotive department knows my wife is going to a counselor?* It felt like there was a huge tattoo on my forehead, "Hi, my wife is in therapy, and I may be the reason. Where are the air filters?" A HIM hides this information from everyone around him. He would much rather tell you he has hemorrhoids than admit that his wife is going to counseling.

I would drive her to the church where the counselor had her office and then walk the streets aimlessly for an hour, wondering what those two were talking about. I thought I was really concerned about my wife and wanted to do the very best I could to reach out to her. Even though I wanted to think I wasn't part of my wife's problem, I planned little things to encourage her. Each week when she'd get back in the car, I would lovingly turn down the volume on whatever game I was listening to (which is a huge thing, because she usually arrived in the late innings), and I would ask, "So, did you guys talk about me at all?" This was my one, overriding concern. *Does your counselor think I'm your real problem?*

I recall several times in the first month of counseling when Andrea smiled coyly and said, "Oh, it wasn't really about you. It was about . . . well, everything. When the time is right, I'll tell you."

This, of course, made me wonder all the more what happened in those counseling sessions. Did the counselor have a big circle with the names of all our family members pasted along the edges? Did she spin a dial and then spend the hour talking about whoever's name it landed on? It sounded like a fun game, unless it was *my* name the spinner chose. Could they be talking about intimate details of our life in there? Was my wife divulging the amount of ketchup I put on my food? Who knew? Only two people, my wife and her counselor.

My desire to know what they talked about pulled me into that office. The humiliation of actually going into a counseling session finally took a backseat to my curiosity. I had to know what they were saying.

If you're trying to get your HIM into counseling, be as secretive as possible about what goes on between you and your counselor. Say things like, "Yeah, and sometimes we just watch a game or two on her big-screen TV." He probably won't believe you, but it's worth a try.

The second thing that really made me want to go to counseling was a phrase my wife threw out one evening over dinner. I remember I had only gone through half a bottle of ketchup when she said, "I was wondering, would you like to come to a session next week?" My eyes bulged. My heart skipped a beat. Thoughts began to race through my head. *Do I have to be vulnerable? Will they use the spinner on me? Will I have to sit and watch my wife cry? What do I do if that happens? Do I put my hand on her shoulder to show I really care, or should I turn and look at the books on the shelf? Do I say the things that come into my head, or should I make up something the counselor wants to hear? What happens if I tell the truth, which is that I would rather be in a meat packing plant, grinding the entrails of a few close personal friends, than sitting on this chair and talking about my marriage?*

Then Andrea said the magic words that will instantly snap a HIM to attention. He loves to hear this sentence.

"She says you might be able to help me with some of my problems."

Help her? Did she say "help her"? Even though she used the word *help*, I heard *fix*. I was going to be the great savior of my wife. Forget all the psychoanalytical theories. Forget all the stages of grief. I was her knight in shining armor, ready to tackle her difficulties with my sword of truth. I was going to ride into that counseling room with only one unselfish desire in my heart: I was going to fix my wife. Even though I had failed to fix her on my own, I would use the neutral setting of the counselor's office to repair my wife's psyche and put her entire world back on an even keel.

Me. The Great Fixini. With only a few words pulled from my pocket of observations, I was going to give insight to the blind and heal the emotionally lame. I had dreams that night of what might transpire.

Wife: I'm really at a loss. I just can't figure it out. Boo hoo.

Counselor: Well, I'll have to admit I'm baffled. In all my years of training and study, I've never come across a case so complex, so difficult to diagnose. You might have to go to a specialist. But before we give up, why don't we see what Chris has to say about it?

Me (dramatic intake of breath): Well, I feel a certain distance when she comes in the room. There seems to be an anger toward other people, especially when I happen to be in that room, and I'm wondering if it doesn't have something to do—

Wife: Yes?

Counselor: Yes?

Me: Well, I wonder if she's not suppressing a need to watch more games on television.

Counselor: (looks on in utter amazement)

Wife: (begins to weep uncontrollably as the truth is revealed)

Counselor: Wow.

Wife: Double wow.

Me: It's a gift.

HIMSPEAK

"Do you know how much money counseling costs?"
Translation: I'm scared to go to counseling.

I was going to counseling for one reason, to fix my wife. And ladies, if you want to get your husband in the counseling chair beside you, let him think that's why you want him there. For it's true that you want his insight. You want his side of the story revealed during a session, no matter how skewed it is. But I know the real reason you want your HIM there. You want him to open up and begin to tell the truth. About himself. This is when the ugly thing begins. This is when your HIM becomes skewered like a human shish kebab. But back to my experience.

On the first day of counseling, I walked in to find there was no television. There was only a desk, a couple of chairs, a couch, and a big box of tissues. This was frightening. Tissues. For crying.

The counselor's name was Linda,* and she was only a few years older than my wife and me. She stood and shook hands with a firm grip, which I appreciated instantly. She smiled and said, "I've heard so much about you."

"I'll bet you have," I said. We all laughed.

She listened a lot and smiled when I'd make a joke. When my quips were really funny, she would throw back her head and bounce on her chair, which made me want to come back every week. She was a great audience. She understood all my jokes. Andrea had been seeing Linda a few months when I finally sat down and began to talk.

I don't know what I expected. I think maybe I figured we would lay hands on Andrea's head and pray for the first twenty minutes. Then the counselor would ask a series of questions that would insightfully show the depths of Andrea's condition. Finally, we would be given homework assignments and come back in a week to repeat the process.

But we didn't do anything like that. We just sat around and talked about Andrea and how she was feeling. We talked about her life, her experiences, her faults, her idiosyncrasies, and her emotional state. We talked about her family, about her relationship with my family, her relationship with her church family and friends, and how she felt about all of those. We talked about how helpful and honest her journal was. I was asked my opinion of certain things. I recall sitting back in the chair, crossing my legs, and spewing forth rich treasures of insight and wisdom as to how Andrea could "get over" all her problems.

*I'll call her Linda because her name is Linda.

Things were going along quite well. Andrea was getting fixed, and I believed I was doing a wonderful job helping the process along. There were a few times when Andrea would reveal certain things in our relationship, such as, "He doesn't do much around the house, and he expects me to do just about everything," but I was quickly able to make a joke or steer the conversation away from me and back to her.

By the way, the only time a HIM wants the conversation steered away from himself is when he's perceived as part of the problem.

One day I felt an incredible ability to help fix my wife. I was being witty and charming and adept at pointing out faults. There was a sense of freedom about the room, because I had finally become comfortable with the chair, the desk, the people, and the reason we were together. I had wonderful insights about Andrea, her friends, and just about everyone in the universe I wanted to change. I was really King Fixit that day.

The counselor stopped the session in the middle of a particularly funny quote I had used to put Andrea in her place. (HIMs put people down to make themselves feel better.) Linda looked at me. In fact, she stared at me, but not in amusement.

I've blocked her exact words from my memory, but I recall she mentioned my tone and called attention to the fact that I appeared to know everything. She confronted me with my arrogance and the times when I tried to be funny when we were talking about serious things.

"Do you know how that makes Andrea feel when you say things like that?" Linda asked.

"Well, I was only kidding. Can't you guys take a joke? Laughter is the best medicine, you know."

"And why do you always have to be funny?" she continued, her eyes boring into my soul. "Why is everything turned into a joke? What are you afraid of?"

This "afraid" question was Linda's favorite. She used it many, many times in my presence, so I immediately went into my next routine.

"How many psychologists does it take to change a baby?" I shot back, wondering why I was paying to have her humiliate me in front of my wife.

Somewhere deep inside, a little boy grabbed his knee in pain and screamed, even though it was his heart that was breaking.

Andrea wept.

The counselor did not smile. Andrea looked straight ahead, except for the times she was grabbing a new tissue. Then that started to annoy me, so I put the whole box in her lap.

I was alone in the chair with myself and my feelings. The room started to close in as I suddenly realized I had feelings. I didn't want to have them. They felt like a whole sack of hot potatoes. I wanted to get rid of all of them, but there was nothing I could say or do to rid myself of those feelings. So I sat in that chair and tried to figure out some snappy way to get out of that situation. The more I thought, the worse my predicament became. The silence was deafening. I heard mice eating cheese three blocks away.

"What do you have to say about those things?" Linda asked.

I point to that moment as the first of some big changes in my life.

126

I realized that day that my wife was not the only one with problems. We both needed "fixing." I probably needed it more than she did. My wife had borne both our feelings and disproportionately carried the emotional weight in the family. I had gone into the counselor's office as a savior and came out realizing I needed one.

That's why it's good for you to go ahead and get counseling if you think you need it, whether or not the HIM in your life will go. If you make some changes in your life, in the dynamic of the marriage relationship, your HIM will have to react to those changes. I was struck by the new power in Andrea's life. She didn't come to me and ask questions about everything. She began to have confidence in herself, which threatened me. She made decisions without even asking my opinion, and that threatened me big-time.

The hour dragged on. My face was flushed with embarrassment. I was sure someone had taped our discussion and I would see it on the evening news. If that didn't happen, I was sure Andrea was going to hold the conversation over me and say, "See, I knew my problem was you!" And with that, my biggest fear surfaced. I really didn't think I had many fears, but as I thought about it, two things surfaced. My first fear was that it would suddenly dawn on someone that I was really a great big jerk. (It hadn't occurred to me that most people had already figured that out.)

But I was even more afraid of losing Andrea's love. You see, no matter what he says, the overwhelming fear in your HIM's life is that you will stop loving him. Not that you will leave him or divorce him or abandon him; those things are awful to think about, as well. But the worst possible event a HIM can imagine is his bride looking into his eyes and telling him she has no love left for him. This is worse than an ax-wielding monster or a three-headed beast from the Amazon. He has based much of his life on the fact that there is someone at home who will love him, no matter how badly he messes up his life.

As I drove home that day, I was surprised to see Andrea look at me with compassion.

"You doing okay?" she asked.

"I didn't know you were going to gang up on me like that," I pouted.

"We didn't gang up on you."

"It sure didn't do much for my self-esteem. I thought counselors were supposed to boost your self-esteem. That's the worst counselor I've ever seen; she's self-esteem impaired. She needs to go back and take that class again. I don't even think she knows how to say self-esteem."

"She was getting you to tell the truth."

"She was getting me to commit suicide."

"She was helping you to see yourself."

"I have a mirror, thank you."

Even though I was defensive and crass, Andrea's tone with me was redemptive, like everything was going to be all right. She still loved me and finally understood how hard it was for me to feel anything. And it felt bad. Really bad. It felt like someone had kicked me in the stomach with hiking boots, and then kicked all my teeth out, and then put my head in a vise and squeezed it really hard until my tongue was the size of Alabama. Then it felt like they drove big spikes into my ears and slammed my spleen on a table and flattened it with a sledgehammer. It felt like an episode of *The Three Stooges*.

But amidst the pain, I saw for the first time that my wife really wanted the best for our relationship. She was willing to go through some intense, emotional trauma for the sake of our marriage, and I will always love her for that.

She had been talking about "being on the same team" for so long that I was getting sick of the sports metaphor. "We're not on the same page, we're not going the same direction," she would say. I realized in that brief moment that I was not enjoying a marriage but a competition. I was engaged in a daily battle to build myself up, and in the process I was tearing her down. If I could keep myself in this constant state of superiority to my wife, no matter what happened with the rest of my day, I felt okay. But it was not okay for her, and the crazy part of it was that she didn't want to win the competition. She wanted to stop the struggle and get on the same team with the same goals and the same agenda. I have no idea why it took me so long to figure this out, or why I still lapse into the competitive mode at times.

HIMSPEAK

"Look, I'll change. It's going to be a brand-new me."
Translation: I'll promise anything to keep from going to counseling.

But I do know the path to healing has been a process. As Andrea and I have moved closer together, I've begun to feel a lot more emotion. You may need to face the truth that your HIM will not have or express feelings the same way you do. He will not react the way you want at all times. This is because God has created you both as unique beings. Do not try to mold your HIM into your own image. He will never think the way you do, and he'll always look bad in a dress.

Your goal in getting him to go to counseling should not be to mold him into something you want. Face it, your HIM may not like your kind of music; he may not show love the same way you do; he may not read many books; and he probably won't enjoy your type of movies. But remember this: Beneath the cool, calm exterior of your HIM may beat a heart that does feel and wants to be on your team. It may take a long time to surface, and it may take more sessions than he would like, but it's there.

Your relationship is worth the pain you may be going through right now. Even if your HIM never goes into a counseling session, your perseverance in working through the issues that haunt your marriage will score many runs, or make marvelous touchdowns, in the future. Take it from someone who finally joined his wife's team. Take it from someone who still wants to play quarterback.

1. Leo Tolstoy, *Anna Karenina*, trans. Rosemary Edmonds (New York: Penguin Books, 1978), 506.

What You Can Do

1. Get counseling if you need it. Don't wait for your HIM to come with you. Go. And don't tell him what happened or who you talked about. This will make him so curious that he may want to talk about it.

2. Ask your HIM questions like, "How does it feel when you watch all those characters get blown up on television?" "How does it feel when I hide the batteries to your clicker?" "How does it feel when I ask you how it feels?"

3. Ask your HIM to tell you one thing he would like to change about you. Let him vent any frustration, no matter how petty. Then tell him one thing you would like to change about him. Start with small things, such as, "I'd like it if you picked up your socks in the morning," rather than, "I wish you weren't so emotionally detached."

4. If all else fails, have a feeling competition. This forces your HIM to have feelings or lose a game, which he is predisposed not to do.

A woman must be a genius to create a good husband.

HONORÉ DE BALZAC

The LORD God said, "It is not good for the man to be alone. I will make a helper suitable for him."

GENESIS 2:18

If a man watches three football games in a row, he should be declared legally dead.

ERMA BOMBECK

Chapter Eight

HIMs Discuss Shallow Subjects

*J*t was four minutes until airtime. My wife was preparing for her program *Midday Connection,* and it was a Monday. On Mondays she talks about marriage. I'm convinced she picked Monday as marriage day because we generally fight on the weekends, and she figured she could get free counseling through her program. Mondays always seem to remind me of how far short I have fallen on Saturday and Sunday.

On this particular Monday she came out of the studio and found me. She had a certain look on her face, her eyes wide with concern, a certain *je ne sais quoi.* (A HIM will try to impress you with other languages, even though he has no idea what certain phrases mean.)

"Our guest isn't here yet," she said, "and we're having problems with the phones. Would you mind helping out with the topic for a few minutes?"

I felt like Brer Rabbit being tossed into the briar patch! I loved the thought of helping my wife with her program, because I was once again "the savior." I was going to be her audio knight in shining armor.

"Sure," I said. "If you think it'll help the ratings, I'll be glad to come in and speak to your audience."

The topic was anger in marriage and how to make it work for you. As usual, we had some unresolved issues from the previous weekend to "work for us," so once we were on the air, I took the opportunity to steer the conversation in a different direction.

"Can I say something here that might help your listeners?" I asked with a smile.

"Sure," she said nervously.

"I think many men will resonate with my feelings here. My wife frequently asks for deeper communication. She thinks I don't talk about significant issues. This is fair, I think. But when I try to talk about something that's important to me, something I think has worth and adds meaning to life, she either doesn't listen or dismisses the conversation as inane. It's almost as if someone has switched her brain to neutral. I get a blank stare and little reaction to anything I say."

Andrea's version of the conversation was something a bit different. She contends that I said something like, "Yeah, uh, I've got something that makes me angry."

"Okay, go ahead."

"Yeah, uh . . . it's like . . . when I try to talk and she won't listen because it's not important. Do you know what I mean?"

However I expressed it, the point was made. A week later a listener from Arkansas wrote about that exchange. This is an actual letter. If this were not an actual letter you would have been informed to turn to another page. Anyway, here goes.

Dear Andrea,

I love *Midday Connection*. One show that especially blessed me was the one where your husband was on while the phone lines were down. I don't even remember the subject, but he said something very profound that has changed my life with my husband. He mentioned how you were not able to appreciate the subjects or areas that were important to him. That hurt him. Boy, was I convicted. I always thought because my husband's subjects seemed shallow to me that automatically made them unimportant. I was very critical—not so much verbally but in my attitude. Now I listen and take a real interest in what is important to him.

Listener Name Withheld Till Notification of HIM

With that I knew I had hit a nerve. And I knew it would make a great chapter in this book, because the principle can aid untold numbers of husbands and wives.

H I M S P E A K

"Did you see that oil is on sale at the auto parts store?"
Translation: Saving money is my real love language.

Wives tell husbands they want deep communication. They want to speak soul to soul. Therefore, when HIMs begin talking about something women deem superfluous, women check out. HIMs are judged as "not deep enough." But wives often don't understand a very important thing: HIMs cannot get to any level beyond "How are you?" until we feel very safe on our own level. This is the good news. The bad news? It may take decades to get to the deep communication level you want with your HIM. Let me give you an example.

I love talking about the plots of movies, books, and television shows. There's something about the way authors and directors weave their stories and depict their scenes that really gives me a charge. I could talk all day about the camera angles in *Citizen Kane*. I could go into the minute detail of what happens to certain characters in Pat Conroy's novels.

My wife sits and stares at me when I do this, as if I'm a clanging cymbal, or speaking in an unknown tongue. She doesn't mind talking about stories and plots, mind you, but she's more concerned with the people in the fiction. She builds a relationship with them, even if they aren't real. This is why I can't get her to watch scary movies. She writhes on the floor and plugs her ears with her fingers at the suspenseful parts of *Lassie*. If little Timmy even walks close to the edge of the ravine, she's out of the room.*

We used to watch reruns of *Little House on the Prairie* when the

---

The only thing that keeps her near is a vigorous backrub I give with a "rubasaurus" we bought at Cracker Barrel.

kids were smaller. Andrea and the girls always got caught up in the daily tragedies of Laura, Mary, and Ma and Pa Ingalls. Someone would go blind or lose a few frostbitten fingers or misplace their homework. It didn't matter the depth of the problem; be it hanging or hangnail, the girls were right there, involved in the emotional fervor.

But I was oblivious to this sentimentality. I didn't care about the relationships. What I really wanted to see, and I had to wait until the final episode, was for the town to get blown up! That's right, at the end of the series the mill, the general store, the church, and every building was filled with dynamite and blown sky-high. What a great episode!

H I M S P E A K

"Did you hear what happened in the game today?"
Translation: Would you like me to share the most important thing in my life?

I could talk forever about the way those buildings exploded and the look on the shyster's face—the one who bought Walnut Grove—when he saw his property in splinters.

"Honey," I'd say, "did you see what happened to the church bell when they pushed the plunger down? Man, it really blew up! The whole thing just went POW!! Did you see that? Wow, what a great ending to a series, huh? I can't wait until they show it again."

"But what will happen to Mary and her husband and all the blind children?" she'd say. "And I'm afraid Alonzo has some issues in his past that he needs to deal with before he and Laura can go further in their relationship."

Women don't think explosions are as important as relationships. Women don't see the inestimable value of talking about dynamite and its effect on Michael Landon's television legacy. They don't consider conversations on these topics as real communication. But ladies, I'm here to tell you, it is.

Yes, HIMs tend to focus on different things than you do. But could it be that we like explosions so much because they take care of problems quickly? If something explodes, you don't have to deal with it anymore. HIMs tend to run from conflict and difficulty in life. Explosions satisfy something deep inside that they can't experience in the real world.

Could it be that those scenes in *Citizen Kane* touch me so deeply because I don't want to end up like Charles Foster Kane, surrounded by wealth and fortune but utterly destitute of friends? You'd have to hang in there a long time for me to talk on this level, but I believe there's some truth to it.

When I describe the incredible way Michael Jordan hangs in the air, switches the ball from right hand to left, while driving through three defenders, and lays up the ball with his left hand with only milliseconds left on the shot clock, I'm describing something very important. When I describe the consecutive-games-without-an-error streak of Ryne Sandberg, or the ball Bill Buckner let go through his legs in the 1986 World Series between the Mets and the Red Sox, I'm talking about issues of vital marital import. This is every bit as important to me as the swag curtains, the carpet, or wall color is to my wife.

The other day I heard Andrea on the phone, talking with a friend who lives a few hours away. They were discussing the color of their living room walls. I'm not making this up.

"Oh Jackie," Andrea said, "I thought you were always a vine person who liked Hunter Green. You've done the whole thing in raspberry? What happened?"

To me, the color of someone's living room is about as important as whether I had my yearly physical exam. I don't care. But it's important enough to my wife for her to make a long-distance call and discuss it at length. This is the same way I feel about my topics of conversation.

I'm not suggesting that you feign interest in what your HIM says. I'm not talking about your stirring the casserole, fiddling with the burner so it's just right, and then saying, "Okay, I'm listening, I'm listening." A HIM wants your undivided attention. He wants you to share this experience that gives him such delight, for he knows he will never play basketball like Michael Jordan, nor will he ever hit or catch or throw like Ryne Sandberg. Those dreams have died. So when he tells you these things, part of him is saying, "Enjoy this experience with me, for a part of me has died inside because I will never do such a beautiful thing."

HIMSPEAK

"I think the gas gauge on the car is on the fritz."
Translation: I'm getting to a whole new level of vulnerability. My gas gauge is really on the fritz.

A HIM may say I'm overanalyzing and I'm just trying to get you to watch a game with him, which is partly true, but that's because it hits a nerve.

If you really listen to your HIM when he gets excited about something you consider mundane, it could revolutionize your relationship. Your HIM will feel valued, nurtured, and at one with you. Plus, you'll learn some really interesting things you never dreamed you would learn. Here are a few examples:

1. Your HIM can explain the nuances of the TV remote, such as the "Previous Channel" function and how to set the time.

2. Your HIM can give an in-depth analysis of why he clicks around at the hint of a commercial message and explain his inborn sense of timing that lets him click back just as the second half is beginning.

3. Your HIM can share why it's important to watch all of the play-off games and not just a few of them.

4. Your HIM can expose the rigors of his day at the office, including why the copy machine at work depresses him so.

5. Your HIM can make noises with his mouth and share how similar they are to guns, cars, or dynamite exploding.

6. Your HIM can help you relive his elementary school days when, strangely enough, he learned to make noises with his mouth that sounded like guns, cars, or dynamite exploding.

7. Your HIM, with enough time and listening from you, can speak to the deep issues of your heart, weep with you, help you work through a nagging problem, and be vulnerable with his thoughts and feelings.

To emphasize this point, I'd like you to picture two different conversations. In the first conversation, a HIM and his wife are having dinner alone. Their children are off together, playing games. The wife starts the conversation with a question.

Her: So, how was your day?

HIM: Oh, okay, I guess. We had that same problem with the coffee maker again.

Her: Hmmm.

HIM: You know I can't understand why they don't invest in a better coffee maker. Coffee is so important to the ambiance of a workplace.

Her: Hmmm.

HIM: You're not listening again.

Her: Oh yes I am. I'm just trying to get this light to come on. I've tried it thirty-five times now and still not a thing.

HIM: Here, let me do that.

In the second conversation, the HIM and his Her have found a better way of communicating. Notice how the Her is able to set the tone for the entire dialogue.

Her: Hi darling, see any games today?

HIM: No, but I thought we might watch SportsCenter together.

Her: Oh goody, I can't wait.

HIM: The NCAA is really heating up!

Her: Ooh! I think I just got goose bumps. By the way, how was your day at the office?

HIM: So-so. We couldn't get the coffee maker to work again.

Her: That's the second time this week, isn't it?

HIM: Mmm-hmm.

Her: That's a real shame. I know how important the coffee maker is to a hardworking man like you. It seems like that company would invest in one that works for a change.

HIM: Yeah, you got that right. But I've been wondering if this coffee maker situation isn't a symptom of my need to control things.

Her: Oh?

HIM: Yes, you know how I sometimes struggle with making other people conform to my way of thinking and how demanding I can be?

Her: Well, no, I didn't know you struggled with that.

HIM: Yes, I do. Hey, why don't we get some light in here?

Her: Sounds good to me.

HIM: Well, this light is driving me crazy; it takes forever to come on. Doesn't it bug you?

Her: Oh, just a tiny bit. But it's such a small inconvenience compared with all the important things you're dealing with. It's really not a problem.

HIM: Still, I'd like to see you have something that works when you need it. Why don't we go down to the lighting store and pick out one together?

Her: I'll get my coat.

HIM: Good.

Her: But, wait. What about SportsCenter?

HIM: We'll stop by the electronic store and watch it on a big-screen TV.

Her: Really?

HIM: Hey, I know what makes you tick, baby.

Do you see how a little bit of listening to your HIM changes the whole dynamic of the marriage? In the beginning conversation, only perceived shallow issues surfaced. In the second conversation, the HIM felt more safe with his spouse, and he was able to bare his soul.

I'm not suggesting that watching sports and listening to his stories will make all your problems go away, or even that you'll get a new light for the kitchen, but you will become more aware of what's important to your HIM. In time you'll be able to break through that tough, crusty exterior and see the gentle, humble servant that is hiding within, and hiding very well.

Either that or you'll start to remember Orel Hershiser's ERA in the 1988 World Series. In my book, neither one is half-bad.

What You Can Do

1. Practice listening to your HIM. Listen so you can repeat what monumentally important thing he has just told you. *Listen.* Take notes if you have to. Make what he's talking about the most important thing in your life for those few seconds he's willing to speak.

2. Practice the careful art of not predicting what your HIM will say or do in any given situation. This is a great frustration for HIMs. Many times a HIM isn't given the chance to change, because you assume he will act like he has always acted, which is probably true. But it's still frustrating. So don't say things like, "I just knew you were going to say that," or, "I figured you wouldn't want to go, so I asked one of my close friends."

3. Watch a film with your HIM that you wouldn't normally choose. At the end he will ask, "What did you think?" Realize that he will think this was the best action-thriller ever. He will not want you to say it was too violent and had a shallow plot and didn't have believable characters. If you cannot think of something positive to say, use something like, "Well, those were certainly fiery explosions!" or "I'm glad I got to experience this with you."

4. Make a list of films you would like to see, or perhaps films that studios could make, that would please you both. Hollywood may be looking for movies like *Little Women Paratroopers, Jane Eyre: First Blood, When Rambo Met Sally* or *The Exploding Bridges of Madison County.*

Fathers, do not exasperate your children; instead, bring them up in the training and instruction of the Lord.

EPHESIANS 6:4

Children have more need of models than of critics.

FRENCH PROVERB

You can discover more about a person in an hour of play than in a year of conversation.

PLATO

Chapter Nine

HIMs Are Either Shadows or Sergeants in the Home

There are four defining moments in the life of a HIM. Birth, death, sports play-offs, and the moment he hears, "We're going to have a baby." In this chapter we'll see what happens in a HIM's mind when he discovers he's going to be a father. You'll see why HIMs are either drifting shadows or drill sergeants.

There are many ways to break the news about parenthood to a HIM. One day Andrea left a note on my office door that said, "Guess who's coming next May?" I thought it was our missionary friends and wondered how we would fit all of them into our home. I turned the piece of paper over to find "#6" written on the back. It was creative and I was happy, but an explosion went off in my head.

I'll have to paint the baby's room. I hate painting. She'll want me to get a new infant car seat. I won't have to paint that. We'll have to go to the hospital. I hate hospitals. I'll have to get another job just to pay for all the baby cereal and diapers. Wait! What is this going to do to our sex life?

When a woman discovers she's pregnant, she immediately prepares for a lifelong relationship with her child. A human being is growing inside her, and she can't wait to get to know him or her. But a HIM, after the initial shock and euphoria, will be more concerned with providing than nurturing.

A HIM thinks about all the duties to come, for approximately three minutes, then goes into denial. He sees your stomach grow, but the reality of the situation doesn't sink in. This is why he doesn't paint the room or get the car seat until the last minute. It's the "Return of the List Factor." If he can put off doing these things, he can stretch the pregnancy into ten months or even a year. *Hey,* he thinks, *elephants do it.*

The big day finally arrives. You say, "I think it's time." He rushes you to the hospital and tries to help in his own HIMly fashion. This means he puts on the gown and turns on the TV. *This will help take her mind off it,* he thinks. Taking your mind off it is his alternative to Lamaze.

Our second daughter, Megan, was born in August 1987. I remember the night clearly because the Chicago Cubs' Andre Dawson hit a home run against his old team, the Montreal Expos. Andrea had just been given a two-liter bottle of petosin, and I was rubbing her back. Cautiously, and with great sensitivity, I turned down the volume on the television remote and clicked to the game. Moments after doing so, Dawson smacked one over the right field wall—one of forty-nine home runs he would hit that year. Megan's birth was an unforgettable experience.

The unforgettable part, however, was not the home run but the sound of the metal bedpan clanging against my skull. I finally realized that she didn't want me to watch the game;* she wanted me to concentrate on her. HIMs have to be reminded of this repeatedly. They also have to be reminded to be very careful where they point the video camera.

"Okay, honey, smile!" I said, as the camera whirred beside my ear. "Turn around a little bit so I can see your face. No, when you hold the bedpan up like that I can't . . ."

Clang!

Then comes the moment a father will really never forget. It's happened to me numerous times, but the experience is always unique, always special. The doctor says, "Look, Papa, the baby's head," and with blurred eyes I look at the child conceived in love, ready to enter the world. The head appears, and the doctor suctions the mouth. Then one shoulder appears, and another. Finally, there it is, all pink and crying.

They wipe the little thing off, clamp and cut the cord, and put the baby on my wife's chest. This tiny person, who made my wife's

Her fingernails digging into my skin really gave it away.

belly so big only moments before, is now crying in her arms. She weeps as she cradles her child. She kisses. She hugs. She nurses.

This is why it's so hard to be a father. I will never know the closeness my wife feels at that moment. I cannot feel the kick from within or the hiccups against my ribs. I will never understand what it's like to nourish a child from my own flesh.

A HIM can merely hold a hand, breathe through a contraction, and watch. A HIM can only pat a back, wait for a burp, and imagine. He will never feel the intimacy, never feel the closeness, and—thank God—never feel the pain his wife goes through.

A HIM can only compare. "I had a kidney stone the size of a robin's egg once," he will say, trying to let you know he comprehends. But he can't understand.

HIMSPEAK

"I'll play a game with you as soon as I finish this."
Translation: If I wait long enough, maybe you'll forget you wanted to play a game.

This is a key reason why HIMs may exhibit distance between themselves and their children. A HIM does not use tissue-tearing force to bring a child into the world. A HIM does not carry around forty extra pounds. (Well, he probably does carry an extra forty pounds if he sits around watching TV all the time, but it has taken a lot more than nine months to put it on.) He doesn't feel what it's like to have to get momentum to roll out of bed.

Since your HIM invests less energy in the birthing process and is less connected physically to the child, he may become detached. You see the child as wet cement; he sees the child as wet cement that needs a name written in it. As soon as he's done that, he leaves.

John Huston's film *Uncle Buck* contains one of the most staggering scenes depicting HIMs in modern cinema.* At the beginning of the film, a young girl laments the fact that boys are so loud.

"Why do we need them anyway?" the youngster asks her older sister.

"We need little boys," the steely-eyed teen replies, "so they can grow up, get married, have children, and become shadows."

This is the way most HIMs respond to children—they become shadows. Distance is a HIM's middle name. A shadow HIM will answer the phone and hear his child say, "Hi, Dad, can I talk to Mom?" When his wife keeps the children, she is a mother, but a shadow HIM who watches them is "baby-sitting." His wife will look through every baby book on the planet before selecting a name. A shadow HIM will choose "Orson" or "Spike" or his own name because it's easy to remember. His wife will take great care when putting her children in the car. A shadow HIM sees the task as a calf-roping

You don't know how long I've waited to write the words "modern cinema" in a book.

151

competition. He wants to throw up his arms and yell, "Time!" when he clicks that seat belt in place. A shadow HIM will take care of the kids only when it makes him look good.

A HIM's wife will want to know every detail of a friend's delivery. Shadow HIMs remember nothing.

"Hey, did you hear?" he shouts. "Jim and Cheryl had their baby!"

"Really? Was it a boy or a girl?"

"Uh . . . I'm not sure."

"How much did it weigh?"

"Oh, 'bout ten or fifteen pounds, I guess."

My greatest fear, and I suspect that other HIMs feel this way, is becoming a shadow to my children. I don't want a distant relationship. I want to be approachable. I want my children to climb onto my lap and tell me all their concerns. I want to know about their best friends and what happened that day and what music they enjoy. I believe most HIMs feel the same way, but they never get around to fostering such a relationship.

Another factor contributes to your HIM's distancing. Inside the mind of most HIMs is a built-in screen saver. When asked, "Dad, could you play a game?" his screen saver kicks in, and immediately he sees flying toasters in the form of unread newspapers and to-do lists a mile long. This is why he stares off into space at inopportune times and responds to his children, "What was that? Uh, yeah, I'll play a game in a few minutes. Sure. Let me finish this first." When the HIM finally finishes whatever was so important, he has grand-children.

A shadow HIM values his children. He thinks about them often on the golf course. He remembers their recitals when he's halfway home from work. But a shadow HIM doesn't have to be miles away to be distant. This is the most frustrating part of living with a HIM. A shadow HIM can be in the same room and still be detached.

Take the story of Mr. and Mrs. Parent. Mrs. Parent (we'll call her Jill) is nursing a baby at the same time her two-year-old is pleading at the top of her lungs for a snack. Jill is also folding three loads of laundry and is mentally preparing dinner, knowing that she has an empty refrigerator.

On the couch opposite her is Mr. Parent (we'll call him Joe), the shadow. Joe is reading a copy of *Popular Parenting* magazine. With his feet up. And a pillow under his head. The title of the article he's reading says, "How to Spend More Time with Your Children." He's really trying to be a good father, and he considers this research.

H I M S P E A K

"No, Son. This is a job for grownups. You'll be big enough soon."
Translation: I don't have time to show you how to work a wrench.

The door bursts open. Two siblings run through, shoes flying, gloves and scarves peeled off like dead skin. The door slams, the baby jerks from the breast and begins to cry, the two-year-old has now opened three packages of peanut butter crackers and has crushed them on the kitchen floor, and the incoming children yell in unison, "Mom?"

Joe is now at the top of page thirty-four, reading, "Quality Time Means Quantity Time."

The schoolchildren descend with lightning accuracy on the exposed legs of Jill while she squirms to get a bit of oxygen to the baby. The two-year-old sweeps the crushed crackers into the metal strip on the sliding glass door. One child picks up a paperweight, and the mother quickly takes it away.

"I was here first," one yells.

"No, I was here first!" the other screams. "Mom, I really have to tell you something."

Jill, who has truly waited for this moment all day, is still smiling at the sight of her children. She wants to give each one just the right amount of attention. The baby gasps. The two-year-old has now opened a five-pound box of raisins—which will present grave consequences for Jill later in the evening—and the verbal battle between the two schoolchildren has accelerated into a physical war.

Jill glances at Joe and sees the back of *Popular Parenting* magazine. Her blood pressure rises because she can't understand why the children always pounce on her while he just sits there.

Finally Joe pulls the magazine down just enough for Jill to see his look of disdain. Then Joe says the fatal words, the words he wouldn't have said if he had read as far as page fifty-three of *Popular Parenting's* edition, called, "Fifty Things Not to Say to Your Wife."

"Can't you get them under control?" he asks.

Later Joe will realize he should have chosen his words more carefully. He will lament the fact that he said, "Why don't you just tell them to get off you?"

Joe, the shadow, has no clue that there is a direct correlation between the little tornadoes swirling about the room and being a father. He thinks he's doing Jill a favor when he volunteers to go to the grocery store just before dinner. As everyone knows, this is peak time for arguments, chores, homework questions, and "the frog effect." The frog effect occurs when a mother can't step anywhere without the child jumping off its own lily pad and onto hers. A HIM does not consciously get out of the house at this hour. He is drawn by the tides to other regions.

Shadow HIMs don't understand children, because they've never taken the time to get into their world. I recall once asking my daughter to pick up her tail as we walked into a furniture store. She was wearing a leopard outfit, and the tail dragged behind her in puddles of water. "She shouldn't be in public like that, should she?"

"She'll be fine," my wife said, smiling.

Shannon gave me that "I'm glad Mommy's here" look, her painted whiskers twitching.

But I realized something important that day. It wasn't my concern for our daughter's reputation that had me frazzled. I was embarrassed by her leopard suit. *Me.* The HIM. I wanted her to put on a nice frilly dress so people would look at her and say, "What a darling child; they must be such good parents."

Instead, thought I, *everyone we pass in that store is going to look at this little urchin and think, "Let's call the authorities. Those people obviously don't know the first thing about raising children."* This was coupled with my fear that the little leopard might dart beneath one of those Broyhill bedroom sets and start growling at the sales staff. Never underestimate the imagination of a child.

I was looking at this shopping trip through my own eyes. I was going to buy a dresser and chest for a bedroom. My daughter saw a detour in the game she had been playing all morning; she was being a leopard . . . thinking like a leopard. It was just another jog along the jungle path.

Shadow HIMs do not know the joy of sitting in a pile of sand and just scooping it for no reason. HIMs are busy. Usually too busy to think about silly things like leopard outfits. If you can break through and help your HIM catch a glimpse of this unseen world, he may become less of a shadow and a lot more fun.

There is another type of HIM father that vexes families. He appears to be the opposite of the shadow HIM, for he is the controlling, smothering military commander. Instead of seeming miles away, the sergeant HIM is always lurking in the background, ready to clamp down on his children like a vise. He gives specific instructions about everything. He tells his children the exact number of times to brush their teeth. He gives precise instructions on how to properly tie a garbage bag. "Stay on the sidewalk. Walk around mud puddles, not through them," he says.

The sergeant HIM hovers around his children like a cobra, ready to strike at any moment, for any infraction of the rules. He is strict about bedtimes, finishing food, and proper attire. He trains his kids like others train their pets.

The sergeant HIM feels very good about his parenting skills. He thinks that by giving rules and regulations, and then enforcing them with an iron fist, he is being a good father. While other kids whine or throw fits in a restaurant, his children sit straight, keep both feet on the floor, and know which fork to use at all times. He thinks he's an excellent father, because he can, on command, make his children obey. He is training them "in the way they should go."

The sergeant HIM, because of his need for control, has a problem admitting fault. He has a syndrome I call, "The Sorry But." Whenever he's caught by his child doing something wrong, he usually dismisses it as insubordination. "Don't challenge me!" he says. But, on occasion, he will respond by saying, "I'm sorry I did that, but if you hadn't . . ." This is the "Sorry But" his children must endure.

H I M S P E A K

"You kids had better shape up or else."
Translation: Heel.

I will admit that, at times, I have the "Sorry But" syndrome. Recently we had friends over for dinner, and I wanted them to see my home office. While I was trying to explain this very important room, my oldest daughter took a beanbag chair and put it on her head.

"Erin," I said, "put that down and go out."

The children's version of a HIM's speech is usually, "You yelled at me." The tone of the sergeant HIM is often like the bark of a bulldog.

An hour later we were in a heated discussion about the scene. Erin tearfully added something that cut to the quick.

"You cared more about what they thought of your office than about my feelings."

I thought about that and sensed through her tears that she really was quite hurt. So I did what any self-respecting HIM would do. I said, "I'm sorry your feelings were hurt, *but* you shouldn't put the beanbag chair on your head in my office."

"You always turn it around and make it my fault," she said. "Why can't you just say you're sorry?"

Good question.

Sadly, the sergeant HIM has no more of a relationship with his troops than the shadow HIM. The children sense he is proud not of them but of himself and his ability to mold them into his own image.

Why do HIMs act in such extremes? Some believe it's the lack of a good example. Most HIMs did not have fathers who actively engaged them in anything but conversation about whether or not they mowed the lawn. They had no pattern to prepare them for parent-ing, and they were much too proud to take a class or read a book. Your pattern was your mother. A HIM's pattern is a shadow or a sergeant.

Your HIM may believe that showing love is equal to providing nice things. *As soon as I get that promotion and a raise, I'll be a much better father, because I'll have more money to spend on my kids.* This, of course, is muddleheaded at best. When your HIM gets more money, he's going to want more things, so he'll work harder and actually spend less time with the children.

Another theory about such behavior is that HIMs are too self-absorbed. A HIM whose life revolves around his career or his hobby will have very little left to invest in his children. This happened to me with our daughter Shannon. When she was five years old, she set her heart on participating in a local parade with a friend.

"We have so much going on," I told Andrea. "Just tell her there's no way we can do it."

"But she's counting on it."

"Then let me tell her," sergeant Chris said in a shadowy tone.

I sat Shannon down and explained exactly why, even though we want to encourage her creativity, she couldn't be in the parade.

"We wouldn't make it back from church in time, and it would be too rushed, and we have so much going on. You understand, don't you?"

"Yes," she said and nodded, "but I can still go, can't I?"

I figured she would forget by the time Sunday came, but that morning she was humming and whistling as she tied her shoes. She had that "I'm going to be in a parade" look about her.

Andrea and I argued until parade time. Shannon was wearing her pretty purple shirt with matching necklace. She was smiling. Excited. It was one of those revelatory HIM moments when there's a breakthrough. Choose your battles carefully and all that.

"Okay," I said. "Go ahead and take her."

I stayed with the baby and read the paper while the rest of the family went to the parade. This was a Sunday paper—important stuff. Actually the real reason I didn't want her to go was because it inconvenienced me and my routine for the afternoon. The parade was only two blocks from our house, but I stayed home.

This is how communism got started, I thought. *Some kid wanted to be in a parade, and the father wouldn't put his foot down, and the next thing you knew, Stalin was marching into town.*

I flipped on the television to our local cable access channel. I saw tumblers and Clydesdale horses and fire engines and local dignitaries. I was riveted. A half-hour later I spied her float. It was a wide shot, but I could see her purple shirt and that smile.

I put the baby in the stroller, ran to the street, and found my wife and kids. They were still waiting. "I just saw her on TV," I said triumphantly, like the whole thing was my idea.

"What was she doing?" my wife asked.

"She was waving and smiling."

I ran another block toward the heart of the parade and stopped under a tree. I wanted to experience this by myself. Her float came by, and it looked like her arm was getting very tired. Then she saw me and beamed. She punched her friend, pointed to me, and said, "There's my dad!"

I ran alongside until she came to my wife and children. She waved proudly to her siblings. My wife took a picture; she had been standing in that spot for two hours. Two whole hours for thirty seconds of this.

"Was it worth it?" I asked.

"Every minute," Andrea said with a tremble.

The parade was over, and the float turned into the Village Hall parking lot. Most everyone had gone home to watch a football game or do weekend things around the house.

And there was my daughter, still waving, still smiling.

This image still touches me deeply, and I believe it hits at the heart of your HIM's distant or overbearing attitude. The truth is, your HIM wants to avoid pain. If your HIM ever really got to know his children as the unique individuals they are, the pain of letting them grow up would overwhelm him. A glance at his daughter on a makeshift float might even cause him to shed a tear. Watching kids grow toward independence is a very scary thing. It's hard for HIMs to pour themselves into these young lives and let them fly away. HIMs hate pain, so we either run from it (the shadow), or we try to control it (the sergeant).

There are a few things you can do to help bring your HIM out of the shadows or take the stripes from his shoulder. Let's go back to my daughter Erin's assessment of dear old dad. She had been hurt and was upset by my "Sorry But." When she poured out her heart and let me know she just wanted to hear me say, "I'm sorry," I got down on the floor, hugged her, and said those very words. You should have seen her the next day. It seemed all the weight had lifted from her shoulders.

The most interesting thing about the conversation was Andrea's involvement. She knows I have "Sorry But" syndrome. She came to me early in the evening and said, "Erin's hurt by something that happened tonight. I think you two should talk it out."

Andrea wasn't against me. She didn't try to play referee. She didn't plead for her emotionally distraught daughter and castigate my insensitivity. She simply got us together, sat back, and watched.

This is perhaps the most difficult thing you will have to do with your HIM. You must allow him to make mistakes with your children. There are times when a helpful word about effective communication is appropriate. Try to keep this for when you're alone instead of in front of the children. Kids have a tendency to gang up on fathers. But I find the more a wife lets her children and their father work out their differences, the stronger their relationship will be.

Don't allow a HIM who is self-absorbed to destroy your joy. Take the kids to a parade even if he doesn't want to go. Go to a park. Pack a picnic. Eventually he may see there's nothing in the paper that interesting, and there's certainly nothing more rewarding than spending time with the rest of his family.

Above all, help your HIM understand life from your children's perspective. Any insight you can give, if communicated nonjudgmentally, will help bring him closer to the father he really wants to be.

What You Can Do

1. If your HIM is too much into his work, too detached from his children, ask him to try this experiment. Have him lie on the floor, facedown on the carpet. Call the children into the room and let each of them crawl onto his back and hang on. Then tell your HIM to "act like Flicka." This will either show him how much fun he's missing or give him indescribable back pain, which might also help him slow down.

2. Secretly videotape a typical day when the kids come home, making sure you get a wide enough shot to include your husband. Show this video to the entire family. Get comments from the children and your husband about the content of the video. Ask questions such as, "Do you think it's fair that your mother doesn't get enough oxygen when you come home?" "What could you tell your father while your mother comes up for air?" "Do you think your father's tone is loving?"

3. Practice the art of hiding. When you hide for any length of time, it will force your HIM to answer the all-important question, "Where's Mom?" After twenty minutes or so, he will be forced to deal with the issue at hand instead of saying, "Go ask your mother."

4. Develop word pictures to help your HIM understand how his fathering style affects the family. Tell him things such as, "When you act like a shadow at home, it's like taking me to an

amusement park with a paper bag over my head," or "When you act like a sergeant around the house, the kids don't feel loved. We never know when the next court martial will occur."

What shadows we are, and what shadows we pursue.

EDMUND BURKE

Thou hast made us for Thyself, and the heart of man is restless until it finds its rest in thee.

AUGUSTINE

O God, you are my God, earnestly I seek you; my soul thirsts for you, my body longs for you, in a dry and weary land where there is no water.

PSALM 63:1

Chapter Ten

HIMs Think Spam Is Spiritual Meat

*C*ompared to women, most HIMs are spiritual pygmies. To prove my point, I've included the following transcription of an actual interview I had with two actual people. Wait. Since this is a Christian book, I must confess I made up the interview part, but the people are real. Okay, okay, I made it all up, but the point is real, all right?

Chris: What is your favorite passage in the Bible?

Woman: It's so hard to choose. I memorized all of Philippians last week, and the first part of chapter two is very special. That's the kenosis passage, you know.

Man: I like the part where that little boy goes out and hits the giant in the head with a slingshot.

Chris: You mean the story of David and Goliath?

Man: Yeah, I think so.

Woman: That's in 1 Samuel 17. And I think it's interesting that David went out and gathered five smooth stones before he went to fight Goliath. Many commentators speculate on the meaning of that. I'm just overwhelmed by God's amazing power in using a little shepherd boy to slay a giant. I have giants in my life too, and God always gets the victory.

Man: I think it's neat that the boy not only killed him but also got to cut off his head.

Chris: Thank you, that's quite interesting. Are there any other parts of the Bible that are meaningful to you?

Woman: Well, the psalms are just wonderful. I love passages that talk about a person longing for God. Sometimes I wake up in the morning and recite all of Psalm 63 before my feet hit the floor. "O God, you are my God, earnestly I seek you; my soul thirsts for you, my body longs for you, in a dry and weary land where there is no water."

Man: Yeah, the psalms are good. Since there are thirty-one of them, I try to read one every day.

Chris: Me too.

Why doesn't a HIM take the spiritual lead in the home? This question is the most vexing—next to his inability to vacuum—that the wife of a HIM faces. She wants her husband to pray with and for her, even if he starts praying with her and wanders off.

A HIM knows that a relationship with God is vital, but he finds himself evading God much of the time. His life is so full of activity and noise that God is an afterthought, a benediction to a day of hard work. He tunes in music or talk shows to cover the emptiness. He finds it difficult to go below the surface and talk about spiritual things with his friends.

Women seem to be more "spiritually minded" than men. They seem to be more open and receptive and have less pride and anger. They exude genuine faith.

Godly women I have talked with totally denounce my observation. They contend there is no difference between men and women as far as spiritual receptivity, and this makes me all the more determined to believe I am right, because I think they were just being humble. Women are, on the whole, more spiritual than men. I can prove it.

H I M S P E A K

"Do you think Bobby's cough is okay?" Translation: I'll stay home from church with Bobby today.

Walk into any church and listen to the singing. Who stays on key? Women. Walk into any church nursery and who will you find volunteering to watch the kiddies? Women. Walk into any women's Bible study and who will you find? Women.

Some men do sing on key, but most of them have music ministries that take them all over the world. These same men would undoubtedly volunteer for nursery duty once a quarter and would put on a wig and try to get into a women's Bible study, because the women are more spiritual and the singers know it!

Not all women are spiritual giants, and not all men are spiritual midgets. Some men do volunteer for clean-up duty, but on average, a woman is more likely to observe the Golden Rule, forgive others, and regard God in her thoughts. On average a man is more likely than a woman to suggest, on a Sunday morning, that the roads are too bad to risk going to church because of all the dew. This is the same man who will sit in subzero weather for a football game.

I speak as one who knows the sad spiritual plight of HIMdom. Many HIMs have sold their spiritual birthrights for a microwaveable bowl of soup. Your HIM has tasted the meat of God's Word and settled for spiritual Spam. Something easy. A conglomeration of holy by-products that never satisfy but keep him thinking he's fulfilling his duties.

He goes to church each Sunday, unless he isn't feeling well or one of the kids has a hangnail. (Isn't it interesting how sensitive a HIM can be about the children's health on Sunday morning?) If someone is sick, he valiantly allows you to go with the other children while he stays home to tend the ill child. What a brick.

This doesn't mean a HIM will not engage on some level in biblical minutiae. If the conversation turns to how many emus were in Noah's ark, or the ratio of Philistines to Chaldeans in the ancient city of Ashkelon, he's with you. He'll argue his points passionately and seem quite spiritual. This is part of his competitive nature. Knowing the Hebrew word for "facial tissue" validates him in some strange way.

But when the conversation turns to living out the faith by loving your neighbor as yourself, honoring others, humbling yourself, and making Jesus Lord of your life, he has little to say. It's one thing to know the number of angels in a legion. It's quite another to articulate the way you live out the tenets of 1 Corinthians 13.

Here is my HIM version of a portion of that passage:

> Though I speak with the tongues of men and of angels, and have not love, at least I've been able to speak in the tongues of men and of angels. You can't have everything.
>
> And though I can understand prophecies and mysteries and have all knowledge, which I really think I do, and have all faith so I could move mountains and have not love, well, if you're looking for the perfect spouse, I'm not it.
>
> And though I give everything away to feed the poor and even give my body to be burned and have not love, I'm sure somebody will criticize me for not building up their self-esteem.
>
> A HIM suffers a little and tries to be kind whenever he can. A HIM does not envy, unless there's a really good reason. A HIM tries not to get puffed up or seek his own way, but you know it's hard to be humble when you're a HIM.
>
> A HIM is not easily provoked and doesn't yell unless someone doesn't live up to his expectations.

A HIM rejoices in nothing but the truth, because he believes he knows the truth about everything.

A HIM believes "bearing all things" means he's supposed to lift the furniture and major appliances. A HIM believes and hopes all things about his favorite sports team. A HIM endures all things except colds, noisy children, and nagging.

When I was a child, I spoke like a child, I understood like a child, and I thought like a child; but when I became a man, I . . . Well, I'm really trying, okay?

Do you see your HIM in that passage? Do you long for your husband to be a more godly man? Do you, at times, wish you'd married Billy Graham? Why does a HIM seem more concerned about the things of earth than of heaven? I believe the answer to these questions is the same reason he's inattentive to marital and family issues. Let me explain.

Have you noticed that your HIM is not as involved in romance and courting now that you've been married a few years? Didn't he used to do little things for you before the wedding day, such as hold the door for you, buy flowers, or stay awake while you were talking? You see, when a HIM says, "I do," he means, "I'm done." In a HIM's mind, he has conquered the Mount Everest of love. He has won the prize. He has finished the marathon. Now it is time to claim his trophy—you.

A HIM looks at his spiritual life in much the same way. At one point he walked an aisle, felt convicted, then confessed, and sealed the deal with a prayer. Flashes of spirituality may spring up here and there, but for the most part he believes the job is complete. He's done his part.

The analogy falls apart when we get to the wedding night and your HIM does something about saying, "I do." Something tangible. Something really, really tangible that he can look back on and say, "Man, that was tangible, wasn't it, honey?" But spiritually, many men never consummate their union with Christ. They don't actively pursue a relationship with Jesus.

Lawn mowers are tangible, too. When they break down, a HIM can take them apart. He can check the fuel line or the head gasket. A HIM can't take his spiritual life apart and figure it out. Besides, a vital spiritual life causes the Christian to have feelings, emotions that tug at the heart. Since these things are foreign to a HIM, he shuns them. He sees church as something you do as an obligation. It makes you feel better only to the extent that sharpening the blades makes you feel better about your lawn mower. He doesn't want to get too involved, or it will begin to sap his energy. He'll have to spend time talking to people in the parking lot, and he'll miss the first quarter of the game.

HIMs also find it hard to pray, because they associate God with their own fathering—unapproachable. *God will be busy. I don't want to bother him with all my little stuff. I'll do this myself. I'll pull up my bootstraps and get on with life. After all, God loves those who help themselves. That's in the Bible somewhere, right?*

The HIM believes this mind-set is very spiritual. He's not leaning on the crutch of religion but taking the gifts God has given and running with them. No need for all this "body" talk. He's a lone ranger, battling evil by himself, on his own terms.

Look at the following conversation.

Her: Honey, I have a question.

HIM: Go right ahead, dear. I'm listening intently.

Her: I would like us to start a family devotion time after dinner each evening. It doesn't have to be anything long and involved, just a thought from Scripture and maybe some conversation about the verse.

HIM: I've been thinking the same thing. Let's start tonight!

Does this sound familiar? I didn't think so. No, a HIM will respond to the idea of family devotions, but he's not willing to invest the mental energy into making it a reality. This is because he doesn't see faith as something you pass along to your children incrementally. It's something you do once by yourself and then move on.

If this is frustrating to you, let me give some helpful advice on how to make your HIM more spiritual.

First, don't try to make him more spiritual. You will fail and may even turn him away from God. But you can do plenty that will make him hungry for what you have in Christ. You can do nothing to *make* him become more spiritual.

Second, pray for him. There is nothing more powerful than a godly woman praying for her HIM. I'm not talking about focusing your spiritual energy on your husband. "Change him now, Lord!" should not be your prayer. If you are attuned spiritually, your prayers won't change your husband, at least not at first. They will change you.

H I M S P E A K

"Isn't it legalistic to do devotions every night?"
Translation: I'd rather not do devotions at all.

When you actively petition the God of the universe for the person you've married, when you bring before the Almighty all the shortcomings you see in your HIM, you begin to see that God desires his time and affections infinitely more than you. You begin to pray for your husband out of a heart of love and compassion, wanting your HIM's best interests.

Then, when you're praying earnestly, listing all his faults and telling God what a sniveling, self-centered life he leads, a still, small voice whispers in that solemn moment with the power of a frying pan to the side of the head. In that moment you realize your own faults, perhaps how you've failed to love your husband as Christ has loved you.

It's at this point that you really begin to love him. Not for what he can do for you, not for the ways he may change and become the man you want, but just because he is. Because he's your HIM.

You must be careful when you get to this stage. You will have the urge to tell your husband way too much about what you've realized. You will tend to say you've been awful in the way you've treated him. You will be transparent and honest, and frankly, he might not be ready for it. If you truly go through such a process, I suggest a conversation such as the following.

Her: Honey, I have something to say.

HIM: I told you I would fix that drawer next week, now—

Her: No, it's not about the drawer. It's about me. It's about us.

HIM: Oh no.

Her: Trust me, it's not bad. I want to apologize.

HIM: Apologize?

Her: Yes. Over the last few days I've been thinking about all I expect from you and how I've been trying to get you to change in certain areas. I just want you to know that I'm sorry about that. I've been looking so much at your problems that I haven't seen my own.

HIM: (stunned silence)

Her: So I just need to say that I'm going to try to work on my own issues and love you as much as I possibly can. I really mean it. I do love you just the way you are.

HIM: Is that it?

Her: Yes, that's what I wanted to say.

HIM: This is about the drawer, isn't it?

Her: (breathes a silent prayer)

Some get to this point and fall deeper into trouble by thinking this will somehow snap their HIM from the spiritual doldrums. Your new commitment to love your HIM is not an end in itself, but a beginning. Ahead is a lifelong struggle to balance the needs and aspirations of your life and your family with the realities of loving a HIM.

In the process of your newfound love, you will see gradual change in the relationship. As you confess your sin and seek to change in certain areas where you fall short, your HIM will notice the difference. You will create within him a certain hunger for your new perspective. He will see the peace you've gained. He will see the contentment you've achieved without his having to change at all.

I speak about these things not to give false hope but because I have seen it work in my own life. I have a wife who has done the very thing I've just written. For years we struggled on the spiritual plane, and we still do a fair amount of struggling. At times it seemed our spiritual plane had engine trouble. Our tray tables were stowed and our overhead bins were secured tightly with the love of God, but we were running into great turbulence. The cabin pressure was dropping and the oxygen masks were nowhere in sight.

My wife had dreams of us becoming a closer, more godly family. I had dreams of getting to church on time. She cared what God thought about our lives. I cared what other people thought. I knew lots about the Bible. I knew I had a relationship with God. But it became easier just to coast on past experience rather than make it a living, vital communion. And when you try to coast on an airplane, you can only get so far before you meet the ground.

The spiritual aspect of life is the bedrock, the center of your existence. If this area is dysfunctional, it will affect every part of your family. It is the instrument panel that contains the guidance capability for everything you say and do. You can have difficulty communicating, make mistakes in remembering important days, and display any other fault in this book, but if you do not have this area under control, your life will be in a continual holding pattern over the landing strip called "contentment."

I saw my wife change toward me in the small things, the mundane things of life. The piled-up clothes on my dresser became less of an issue. Then I saw her go through a deeper inner change, and it made me desire what she had. (Actually it made me want to compete with her.) Now, I'm not saying we have devotions every night. We don't pray together as much as we should. The children don't know all the kings in the Old Testament alphabetically. But we're closer to being on the same team, with the same goals, because we have the same Father drawing us ever closer as we get closer to him.

Let me give one practical example. The birth of our sixth child made our three-bedroom house seem even smaller. As one friend put it, we have to go outside the house to change our mind. The baby is in the bedroom, the other children are bunched up, and one child even sleeps on a hook in the closet. (It's a very nice hook with lots of breathing room. No, this is a Fabry-cation.) The considerations for a new place are endless. There are always bigger, better houses.

But when we sat down and analyzed our goals, one question bugged us both. How would moving affect the kids? They loved their schools and the neighbors. There were lots of ways to minister in our racially diverse neighborhood. Plus, we both wanted to plant some roots for the kids so they could come back years later and say, "This is the house where I grew up. This is the tree I fell from. This is where the phone cable is buried that my father kept digging up to put in the swing set. Look (sniff), the hook where I slept."

HIMSPEAK

"I think we should start a couples' Bible study in our home."
Translation: I think you should start a couples' Bible study, and I'll show up once in a while.

We could move to a bigger place with nicer things, but that would affect the dynamic of the family. It might cause us to give less money to the things that matter most. It might reinforce the mis-nomer that contentment comes with the "bigger and better." Compared with most of the rest of the world, we live in a palace! God wants to give fulfillment in our relationship with him and with others, not necessarily give us more bathrooms.

Not to say we won't move if we find a reasonably priced

five-bedroom home next week. There is nothing inherently spiritual about living like a sanctified sardine. My point remains that you can be content in whatever situation you find yourself. And no one modeled this before me better than my wife. If she can be content with me, she can be content in any situation.

If your spiritual life with your HIM is vitally important to you, and only mildly important to him, hang in there. Keep praying. Keep living a godly life. Keep setting a good example before him and your children. Keep setting a good example before others in your church family. Stay humble. And remember, a woman is usually more spiritual than a man, on the average. I can prove it.

What You Should Not Do

1. Do not leave open Bibles lying in strategic places around the house, such as in his golf bag, inside the weekly TV listings, or in the refrigerator.

2. Do not pester your pastor to pester your husband. This leads to two frustrated men.

3. Do not weep and wail or gnash your teeth in prayer about your husband's condition. I know women who have gotten on their knees and prayed out loud for their husbands to become more godly men, and it didn't work. Especially at 3:00 A.M. If you like, you may rend your garments. This is fine. A HIM enjoys a rent garment or two every now and then.

4. Do not pray psalms such as, "May he become food for jackals." Rather, pray Psalm 51:10 and keep a journal of the ways God is changing your heart toward your HIM.

Men bury themselves with responsibility.

WILLARD HARLEY

Marriage halves our griefs, doubles our joys, and quadruples our expenses.

UNKNOWN

Whenever I date a guy, I think, Is this the man I want my children to spend their weekends with?

RITA RUDNER

Chapter Eleven

HIMs Treat Work as Their Significant Other

*L*et's take a look inside your HIM's mind as he gets ready for work.

Boy, this shower feels good. I could stay in here all day. I don't want to go back to work. Why did God create Mondays? Where's my shampoo? Who took my shampoo? I can't believe she would let the kids use my shampoo when I've told her specifically that stuff is expensive.

Well, I'm just going to have to get out of the shower and find out if she let them use the shampoo. I'll use my distressed voice. "Honey?!"

Wait. There's the bottle of shampoo in the trash. That's right, I used the last of the shampoo yesterday, didn't I? And I was going to make sure I put a new bottle in the shower before I left for church, but I must have forgotten.

"Oh, hi honey! No, nothing's wrong. I just wanted to see if you could get me a bottle of shampoo, but I got it. Thanks for coming all the way up here. What? Who, me? Accuse you? No, really, I wasn't accusing you of anything."

She didn't buy it. She knows I think she let the kids use it, and now she's going to be mad at me. Speaking of mad, Harold is going to hit the roof when he sees the sales figures for the fourth quarter. Not good. I don't care if they fire me, I did my part. I'm going to stand up in that meeting and tell them there was no difference in the way I worked in the third quarter than in the fourth. It's just that we hit a record high in one and a record low in another.

I love this shampoo. This feels really good. When I was a kid, I used to put the fluffy shampoo in my hand and make little animals out of it and then watch them disappear in the water. But now my hair is coming out in big clumps. I'm going to look like Werner Klemperer on Hogan's Heroes *by February. I need Rogaine or something. Maybe a transplant. Oh, but what does hair mean, anyway? It's not important. I'm not going to base my worth on how much hair is on my head. No sir. But at least I have more hair than Karl. What a cue ball.*

Okay, what shirt today? Let's see, is there anything I hate more than getting dressed? Hmmm, I wonder if this goes with these pants. Maybe this striped tie will pull it all together. I should just invest in a bodysuit you can zip from the floor so all I'd have to do is put on new socks every day. Would that be great or what?

"No, I don't have time for breakfast. Got a big sales meeting this morning about the fourth quarter. Hi, kids."

I don't want to get any jelly on this tie. I'm ready to go, I'm in my work mode, I have to pull the car out of the garage . . . oh no, I forgot to take the trash out last night. Argh. I just wanted to come through here without interruption and get to work.

Oh no, there it is. The three-by-five-inch card on the refrigerator. Every time I look at that card I think of all the things she's asked me to do that I haven't done. Instant guilt. Do I dare pick it up? Might as well see what's been added in the last twenty-four hours.

Faucet in kitchen

Drawer in kitchen

Light in living room

Lights in family room

Light in kitchen

Hole in living room rug

Tub of water in basement?

This list is almost as old as I am. She's been asking me to fix that faucet for years. I'll tell you the problem; there isn't one. We used to have this water purifier thing on there, and when it stopped working, I just pulled the hose off the doohickey, and now she says it sprays everywhere when she turns the water on, but it doesn't spray when you turn it on right.

The drawers in the kitchen are the same drawers they put in this house twenty years ago. Everybody's drawers are falling apart. It's not like we're alone in this. I'm sure not going to pay thousands of dollars . . .

Would you look at the time? "Bye, honey, I gotta go!"

Lists. Makes me want to avoid the refrigerator. It's hard enough to keep the car in working order and mow the grass, let alone do all the things around the house that need fixing or shingled or cleaned or tightened or bought or thrown out or moved or polished or replaced.

Traffic. I hate traffic. But at least the drive gets my mind washed out. I think I'll turn on the radio.

(Fifteen minutes pass without a thought.)

I wish I had a cell phone to call these yahoos on the radio and tell them a thing or two about baseball. That would be a good thing to do with the kids, take them to a game this year. Maybe next week, yeah, next week I could get a few tickets and take them by myself, give my wife a day off and just take them. What a great idea.

Ooops, I walked out without taking out the garbage. Great. Now she's going to be mad at me because the whole garage is going to smell like cabbage and diapers.

Why do they let jerks like this guy have a license? I think I'll speed up and try to cut him off before he exits.

There. That showed him. Ha ha. Hi, buddy. How's it feel, huh? Jerk.

I should have thanked her for offering me breakfast. What a dodo. I just went by in my own little world. I forgot to ask what she was doing today. Is today the dental appointment? I'll have to call her when I get to the office and apologize.

But I'm not going to apologize to my boss for the fourth quarter. I did as much work if not more than in the third quarter, and it just didn't work out the same. Go figure.

(Listens to the radio for ten more minutes.)

Why do I listen to this garbage anyway? It just gets me more upset when I hear people talking about things they don't understand.

There's a light store. You know, I could pick up a couple of new lights and surprise her when I get home. I'll just throw the one in the living room away; it's no use trying to fix it. I'd just electrocute myself and in my last conscious moments feel guilty I didn't buy her a new one.

H I M S P E A K

"I can't believe how stupid people can be." Translation: I'm depressed about work.

Hey! He did it again. Cut me off twice in one morning. What a jerk! Here's my exit. I hope I get a good parking place.

I ought to pay more attention to the things around the house. If she did my laundry like I do her lists, I wouldn't like it.

I really ought to call and apologize when I get to work. What a jerk I am. You'd think I could see this after so many years of doing it the wrong way. Yeah, I gotta call her and tell her I understand what she's saying. I do care about stuff at the office more than the stuff at home. I need to call her. Right after the meeting. I'll call right after the meeting.

These are the typical thoughts of a typical HIM who works a typical job in a typical town. Notice he has little calculation in his life. For example, he doesn't think, *I have to impress the boss today with my performance.* He would contend that his family is the most important part of his life. He would never cheat on his wife. He would never do that to his children. He is committed.

But his actions say that this man's work is his significant other.

He pours more of himself, his time, and energy into his personal information manager than in raising the kids. To him, work equals satisfaction. Work equals fulfillment. You can see it in his eyes when he talks about a big deal that closed or fell through.

He would disagree. "Well somebody has to pay the bills! We can't all stay at home with the kids."

But he doesn't see himself as you do. He's a HIM.

A few years ago some guys were sitting around a table, trying to figure out how they could be less involved in the home. These were not ordinary HIMs; these were radical, deviant HIMs who were bent on wreaking havoc not only with their own homes but with the homes of millions of people all around the world.

"Let's make a stunningly beautiful robot," one said.

"Won't work," another said. "We tried that last year, and my wife kept reprogramming it to do laundry."

"How about a super subatomic particle fishing rod?" another said.

"Casting all the way to the Aegean Sea would be great, but how do you reel it in?"

"Good point."

These grinchly HIMs thought and thought until the head of the group (you could tell, because he had the most pens in his pocket protector) stood and declared a breakthrough that would be felt around the world.

"Gentlemen," he said, "we're going to give our fellowman something that will consume his every waking moment. He will go to sleep thinking about our invention. He will dream about it. He will compare his to others in the office. He will constantly use this invention and have to have every bell and whistle added to it. And the best part is, every few months the one he has will be obsolete and he'll have to go buy another one. Then we'll convince him he doesn't need just one for his work, he'll also need one for home. We'll make him think it will enhance his family life, when in reality it will sap every ounce of energy from him. We'll not only be rich, we'll be the obsession of every red-blooded male in the universe and the curse of all red-blooded women who wish their husbands were more involved with the family.

"Gentlemen, I propose today that by the year 2000, we will take over the minds of men (and some women) on the planet. And we will do this with our brand-new invention called the personal computer!"

I'm not sure if it actually happened this way, but it doesn't really matter. The computer has become the mistress of the HIM. He can draw with a computer, communicate with friends, rewrite reports, work on spreadsheets, play games, download, upload, and do it all while watching a screen that looks an awful lot like a television. Wives who are computer illiterate are kept at a distance by an incomprehensible language. Wives who are computer literate are just kept at a distance. (You might wipe out his hard drive.)

So I've composed a poem for those of you who see yourselves as computer widows. It's called "Man in a Trance."

There he sits, eyes cast on the vivid screen

while I stand at the edge of destruction,

not knowing the difference between RAM and

ROM.

I tell him, "I need . . ."

He says, "Just let me close this application

and get my e-mail and I'll be done.

It'll only take a minute."

But it doesn't take a minute. It's taking a

lifetime.

How long can he sit there, clicking and typing

away

at that thing, that monster, that mistress of the

dark?

I do not need massive amounts of

attention.

I simply need a sledgehammer and the

fortitude

to smash his Mac into a billion pieces.

But he'll just get another. He has fifteen

already.

A laptop, a desktop, a notebook, a

subnotebook,

a personal information manager, and a few
  PCs.

He's minimized his home life and maximized
  his windows.

His hard drive.

His hard drive, my foot.

I used to think his mouse was cute, but now I
  loathe it

as I watch its tail snake across the cushioned
  pad.

If I had a built-in keyboard where my navel
  rests,

I would ask him to change my auto.exec.bat
  file right now.

"Initialize my modem," I would say. "Log on to
  my chat group."

But I don't know the right lingo,

and I don't have the guts to interrupt him.

Perhaps this is the last click,

the last flick of the "Master Power" that signals
  it's over.

I want to hear the blessed sound of his CPU
  whirring to a stop.

But I do not.

I am a computer widow.

Believe it or not, your HIM actually thinks he's at home when he plays with the computer. In his mind he's patting himself on the back for doing this. He thinks, "I could be playing golf. I could be over at Joe's house watching football. I could be watching television with the kids, which she doesn't like. But no, I'm here on the computer, nourishing my mind, gaining new perspectives on life, and doing it all for pennies a day."

The computer is a safe friend. It never confronts him with all those things he's forgotten to do. The computer even backs up all his files for him, so he doesn't have to think about it. The computer offers companionship and entertainment and that certain feeling of unexplainable excitement HIMs have when they merge the desire to play with expensive electronic equipment. The computer offers contact with real people, but at a distance. He doesn't have to shake anyone's hand, doesn't have to respond to anyone's emotion, and a message is only a delete key away from being toast.

HIMSPEAK

"I'm not going to put such a priority on work anymore."
Translation: I won't bring work home with me until tomorrow night.

Computers are another way to produce noise in the life of a HIM. Something to occupy the empty space. Computers aid in the cocooning of the HIM, wrapping him in cyberstrands of empty chatter.

You rightly ask the question, "Why?" Why does your HIM spend so much time involved in work, so much time on the computer, so much time doing even good things—at church, in the community, for neighbors? Why will your HIM volunteer to help dig up a friend's septic tank when he won't even change the nozzle on your showerhead? What is it that causes him to schedule his life so that every conceivable second is used for something other than what you think it should be used for?

Let's visit the garden again. Picture what it must have been like for Adam and Eve immediately following their banishment from the perfect home. Imagine living just outside paradise, knowing you've blown it, not only for yourself but for your children and their children and all children to follow. Adam, who was not a HIM until the Fall, awakened each morning and thought of what could have been. With each seed planted, with each child birthed, Adam and Eve understood the consequences of their actions.

"Eve?" Adam said, rounding a bush. "There you are. Have you seen the boys?".

"Not since this morning. Why? Is something wrong?"

"No, it's just a feeling. I wish someone would hurry up and write a book about tough love. Abel's fine, but I don't know how to raise Cain."

"Adam, he's a firstborn. I keep telling you birth order really makes the difference."

"I just think something bad is going to happen."

"Oh, you worrywart! Give him a couple hundred years; he'll turn around."

"Maybe you're right. I just see so much of myself in him."

"So, Adam, how's your day going?"

"Same old, same old. Work, work, work. The planting, the plowing, the weeding, the thorns, the thistles. I'm drenched with sweat from sunrise to sunset. There's no hardware store, no power tools. I'm telling you, it's nothing like it used to be. You know, if you hadn't listened to that serpent I wouldn't—"

"There you go, bringing up old stuff again. I thought we weren't going to talk about the garden anymore. You never affirm me. My self-esteem is the pits. You're not speaking my love language."

"I didn't even know you had a love language! You asked me how my day was, so I told you. I'm sorry. I feel a little resentful about sweating my life away while you lounge around the house all day."

"Lounge around the house? You call this hole in the wall a house? Life for me isn't a bowl of cherries, you know. I'm still getting over my last delivery. And you know who's responsible for that!"

"I thought we weren't going to bring up past things . . . "

"Plus I have to raise these boys with an absent father."

"Absent?"

"Yes. You're always in the field. Gotta plant this, Eve. Gotta harvest that, Eve. You never have enough. It's always just one more field, one more orchard. One of these centuries you're going to wake up and see your kids are gone."

"If I don't bring in the grain and food, who will? Answer that one, little Miss Fig Leaf."

"Work is bad enough. Then when you get home, you plop in the chair, and the next thing we know you're asleep."

"You don't know how hard work is," Adam said, his voice cracking with emotion.

"The way to communicate love to me is by acts of service—doing things for me around the house. Your primary love language is—"

"Okay, that's enough! I've got enough guilt as it is."

"Adam, I was just ribbing you. But you know what, we sure could use a marriage enrichment seminar."

"Right," Adam said sarcastically, "we could use a time machine so all this wouldn't have happened, but we don't have that either. I think you've got too much time on your hands."

"You know, sometimes I think . . . Oh, never mind."

"I hate it when you do that! Finish your sentence!"

"Well, I wonder if we can ever go home again? Back to the garden. Will we ever get back into God's presence?"

"And how do you think that's gonna happen? He threw us out of paradise and left his angels guarding the entrance. That's a pretty clear message if you ask me."

"I know, but he was so nice. Don't you think he'd let us back in if we did something really good. If we baked him a cake maybe, or a pie? That's it, I'll bake him an apple pie."

"Eve! You want to get us killed? The boys use your cooking to scare away the wild animals! Look, God is holy. The whole reason we're on this side of the garden is, he's holy and we're not. All it takes is one wrong thing, one bite of fruit—"

"I thought we weren't going to talk about that."

"It seemed appropriate."

"You were there with me."

"You made me eat it."

"I was only offering a bite. You ate the whole thing."

"Stop it, this is getting us nowhere. The point is, we can't go back. There's no way for us to get in, and if we did get in, we wouldn't be accepted. Face it, we are separated from God. Unless he does something to bring us back, paradise is only a memory."

Adam's and Eve's lives were perfect. They had human companionship. They had a divine relationship. They had meaningful work, opportunities for true joy and satisfaction. Everyone and everything lived in harmony. They had an unlimited food supply with no checkout lines. Work and home were not separated; they were one and the same. They didn't have to worry about spending quality time with each other; all time was quality time. Religion was not just for Sunday morning; God was available every day.

There was no separation of the secular and the sacred. There were no neighbors to keep up with, no one to impress. There were no wars. They had peace. They had it all. All except what HIMs desire today.

One thing eluded their grasp: They were not God. They did not have God's knowledge and abilities. They had the most beautiful setting ever created as their playground and the most loving and all-powerful being in the universe as their friend, and still they wanted more.

This is your HIM. In his search for contentment and peace (the garden), he desires to rule his world, dictate the order of events in his little slice of humanity, and give punishment to those who offend. (Actually, we all want to be God, but we're talking about HIMs right now.)

If I were God, a HIM thinks, *I would be able to right the injustices, feed the poor, clear the bad drivers off the roads, speed up the traffic lights, make the drive-throughs fill my order accurately, stop political correctness, and generally make the world a place where people would like me and have fun getting to know me. The world would be at peace, and contentment would fill the land.*

A HIM finds he cannot control all the events and people in his family. So he goes in search of something he can control, and that's why work is so important. There he can be a god. Truthfully, every problem, from communication to insensitivity to inappropriate belching, hearkens back to a HIM's desire to be God. When a HIM belches and is called to account, what he's really thinking is, "If I were God, I'd belch anywhere I wanted and people wouldn't be allowed to complain."

HIMSPEAK

On phone at 5:00 P.M.: "Hi, honey. How was your day?"
Translation: I'm going to be late for dinner again.

In one sense, this desire is a wonderful sign. Your HIM is on a search for fulfillment, peace, and contentment. If he ever stops trying to be God and starts serving God, it's going to be so wonderful that he's not going to want to go back to his former ways.

This is where you come in. If you really wish your HIM would not make his work such a priority, and become a godly man filled with peace, you must show him peace. You must put it before him like a platter of succulent fruits and vegetables. You must wave it under his nose and let the aroma waft toward him like a well-cooked steak. Make your HIM hungry for real peace.

How do you do this? You must possess it. You can't waft what you don't have; and if you don't have peace, there's only one place to get it. Go to God. Then bring the peace you have to the relationship. Make your home a little bit more like the Garden of Eden every day. (No snakes, please.) Follow hard after God, search the

Scriptures, lean on heavenly understanding, and you will be so filled with peace that your HIM won't be able to stand it.

Picture your HIM on his deathbed. Wait, stop smiling; this is serious. When your HIM gets to the end of his life, he's not going to care about fourth-quarter earnings. He won't wish he'd spent more time at his computer. He will wish he'd spent more time with you and the children. He will wish he'd put a priority on the things that give lasting fulfillment. Your task is to get him to see this point without preaching. I suggest the following conversation:

HIM: I have to get some things done tonight for work.

Her: Oh, take as much time as you need. I'll drive Tim to his baseball game. (Turn on Harry Chapin's "Cat's in the Cradle" as low background music.)

HIM: That's right. He was supposed to start at third base, wasn't he?

Her: Don't you worry with it, hon. I'm sure when he's in the major leagues and someone asks who helped him get so good, he'll remember to mention you.

HIM: You know, I think I did enough at the office today. This stuff can wait until later.

Her: Great! I'll just turn off the tape player, and we can all go.

There is real hope for HIMs who work too much. There is a future for women whose husbands are glued to the Internet. There are honest answers for those who have questions, but they are not easy answers. There are no quick solutions that will bring lasting peace.

Sometimes the process will be difficult. But if you're willing to walk through this frustrating maze with your HIM, he may say the words you've been waiting all your life to hear. We'll talk about those in the next chapter.

What You Can Do

1. Tell your HIM you understand how he feels when he leaves for work each morning. Promise him you'll keep the jelly away from his tie if he'll sit down for five minutes and talk before he leaves.

2. Do not, I repeat, *do not* ask your HIM if he would like to be God. He will only look at you and say, "Have you been reading that Fabry book again?"

3. Role-play Adam and Eve before the Fall. Wear realistic attire. What would you talk about? Discuss the issue of peace. Smack your HIM and tell him to look you in the eye when you're talking to him.

4. Ask your HIM to honestly evaluate the amount of time and energy he spends on his work. If he spent as much time with his family as he did at the office, how would his family turn out in ten years?

Love doesn't just sit there like a stone; it has to be made, like bread, remade all the time, made new.

Ursula Le Guin

You can turn a painful situation around through laughter. If you can find humor in anything——even poverty——you can survive it.

Bill Cosby

God has brought me laughter, and everyone who hears about this will laugh with me.

Sarah, Genesis 21:6

Chapter Twelve

HIMs Never Say the Words You Long to Hear

He ain't gonna say it. The last thing a HIM will say is "I'm sorry," unless he's just sorry he was caught. A true HIM will never say "I'm sorry" and really mean it. A true HIM will say "I'm sorry" and then tack on a few words that negate what he just said.

For example, here's a true experience that happened not long ago. My wife would rather pick up a poisonous snake than watch television, so it was fun to watch her become enamored with Olympic gymnastics. She was so excited about the competition. She only gets this excited about skating, gymnastics, and watching John Tesh bang about the piano in a rocky outdoor theater.

Well, to be honest, there were much more exciting things than Olympic gymnastics on television that very evening. There was a re-run of the *Beverly Hillbillies*, the one where Jethro tries to shoot himself into space from the cement pond; there were several movies that looked good, such as *The Leech Woman* and *Jaws 15*; and there was a PBS documentary on the pets of Warren G. Harding. All these shows looked better to me than a bunch of underweight girls hopping around on a padded floor.

But I bit the bullet and graced my wife and children with my presence. I even went so far—now hold on to your pommel horse—I went so far as to let my wife control the clicker. No flipping around during commercials! I could have gone just about anywhere else in the house I wanted and, in retrospect, probably should have. But I decided I would sacrifice and spend time with them as they enjoyed this sporting spectacle.

Unfortunately, I could not hold my tongue when the balance beam competition rolled around. There's just something about running full tilt and jumping onto a six-inch piece of wood that brings out the humor in me.

"Oh no, I'm gonna fall," I said. "Bela, can you get me a bigger beam?"

"Stop it, honey," my wife said. "I really want to see this."

When the girls got to the uneven parallel bars and did those big loops, I would say, "Oh, I think I'm gonna be sick."

"Honey, please?" she said.

As other contestants from around the world competed, things turned worse. I tried to speak with their accents. I did my best Russian, Ukrainian, Romanian, and Chinese. I pretended they had just gone to a fast-food restaurant, and I imitated their orders. It was truly stellar work. My wife did not laugh.

As the evening wore on, the whole competition became much more interesting and funny to me. But I should have seen my wife's muscles tensing. I should have noticed that she plugged her ears when I talked and looked at me as if I had clicked to *The Leech Woman* in the middle of the last vault.

Finally she leaped up, turned off the television, and ran upstairs. I can't remember her exact words, but it was something like, "You knew how much this meant to me, and you still wouldn't quit!"

If I'd had any sense at all, I would have embraced her right then. I would have said the words she longed to hear. "Honey, I'm sorry. I've acted like a little kid while you were watching something you really cared about. Please forgive me. Come back and I'll prove to you I can respect your feelings on this. Please. I'm sorry."

But I did not say those words. All I could think to do was to laugh very hard and say, "Hey, come back. They're gonna do calf roping after this! Come on, honey. Can't you take a joke? I was just having fun. Can't a guy have some fun every now and then? You don't like to have fun, do you? That's your problem; you're too stiff! Your humor muscles need a massage!"

I did what HIMs the world over do. I put the problem back on her. I blamed. And I continued to blame. I could not see the error of my way. The children were screaming that I had messed up their evening, my wife was in tears, and all I could think to do was laugh at the way the announcers talked. Come to think of it, John Tesh was one of the announcers, and I believe I humorously suggested he should go back to banging on his piano by some big rocks.

Why was it so hard for me to say the words my wife longed to hear at that moment? Why does your HIM rationalize his behavior? Why does your HIM blame others for his mistakes?

There are many answers. But the main one is that a HIM believes, wrongly of course, that if he says he's sorry about one thing, he'll have to say he's sorry for everything. This is the principle I call the "List Factor." When you make a list of things for your HIM to do, he looks at it quite differently than you do. You are thinking, *Here are a few things around the house I need done, which I can't do. I could hire someone to do them, but you don't like my hiring people to do things you can do. So I'm making this list so you'll know I would really appreciate your getting around to fixing or doing these things.*

Your HIM holds this wretched piece of paper in his hands and trembles. It is not readily apparent to him what he should think, and he would never admit he's thinking this, but subconsciously he says to himself, *If I do all the things on this list, there is just going to be another list to take its place. But if I don't do the things on this list, the list will stay the same until such time as my wife comes to me in tears about the faucet or the light or the toilet constantly running. When she really starts to nag me about such a thing, then I will do it. This way she'll only be able to put one thing back on the list rather than a bunch of things.*

Your HIM looks at saying the words "I'm sorry" in much the same way. He thinks, *If I say I'm sorry for messing up her evening of watching gymnastics, I'll be admitting that I'm wrong. I'll be saying I'm weak, and I don't want her to think I'm weak. I have to be strong for her. That's what she wants. If I say I'm sorry for this, what will I have to say about the things I said about her meat loaf last week, or the comment I made to our neighbors about her sleeping like a pretzel? I won't be able to say one sentence without apologizing.*

A HIM is afraid to talk on a deep level, because he thinks the ten minutes will turn into an hour, and you'll expect this every time. If he says he's sorry once, he'll have to keep saying it over and over again, and really mean it. A HIM will think in this circular manner all his life unless some drastic change is made.

Another reason a HIM does not want to say he's sorry is that he thinks you will love him less if he admits he's wrong. In his mind he's right unless he's proven wrong. Therefore, you could absolutely hate him for something he did, but if he thinks he did nothing wrong, you're the one with the problem. If, however, he admits to sinning against you, if he genuinely confesses and asks you to forgive him, he is openly admitting to you that he is without excuse and he believes there's no reason for you to love him. I hope you're getting this, because it's really important. A true HIM believes your love, like his own feeling of significance, is always based upon performance. You can't love him just for who he is, because it's not logical. You love him for what he does. You love him for his accomplishments and achievements. If he says the magic words "I'm sorry," he has torn away all the reason you have to love him. He feels alone. Undone. Unworthy. This is why, no matter how bad the infraction against you, your HIM will always make it someone else's fault. Instead of saying, "I'm sorry," and stopping there, he will say, "I'm sorry, but if you hadn't . . ."

The positive thing about the List Factor is that your husband truly desires your love. If he didn't care for you and crave your affection, he wouldn't act in such a stupid manner. Does that make you feel better? Of course not, because sin is sin. When someone wrongs you, it doesn't matter what was going on in his or her mind; it hurts.

But it may be helpful for you to know that many HIMs are never able to say those words, but will, with their actions, prove they understand and want to change. So would you rather have someone who says the words and doesn't follow through, or someone who can't say the words but alters his lifestyle? I know, you would rather have someone who changes and can say the words and finish the list, right?

To be honest, the reason your HIM doesn't say he's sorry is because he is sinful. He has his own interests and his own pride at stake. If he were to say, "I'm sorry," and not add something to the sentence, he would be saying, "I did that which was not right, and I open myself up before you now and ask you to forgive me." A HIM cannot do this, because he is taught, from infancy, that is something he should never do. A HIM must be strong. A HIM is supposed to be a leader. Admitting he is wrong is a sign of weakness. Confessing guilt is not a manly thing to do. It means he is not in full control.

There's one exception to this phenomenon, of course. There is that breed of HIM who apologizes for everything, who says, "I'm sorry," at the drop of a hat but never changes his actions. It's almost as if he has his fingers crossed behind his back when he says it. "I'm sorry for demeaning you. Please forgive me . . . you nag. Ooops, I'm sorry I called you a nag. I shouldn't have done that. Can you ever forgive me?" This HIM says the words but still punishes the one who drags it out of him by continuing in the same behavior.

These are the reasons a HIM will not speak those blessed words. May I stand in for your HIM and say the things he cannot express but has needed to say for years? Oh, there are some who might not feel what I'm going to say. They have neither the inclination nor the guts to admit some of these things. But if I'm correct, there are many HIMs who would love to communicate on a deep level but just don't know how. So, if you would, allow me these few words from the heart. Imagine these words coming from your HIM. Perhaps they truly are.

An Open Letter from Your HIM

I have put off writing this letter for such a long time that I scarcely know where to begin. So much has gone unsaid. So many things I should have expressed are withered and gone. If I could, I would do things differently.

Sometimes when I'm in the car, I find myself thinking of you. Or behind the lawn mower—the one you bought at the garage sale and had someone put in the back of the car so that it scratched the backseat. Remember that? The one I got mad at you for buying because it was electric, and I wanted to buy a new one. The one I said wouldn't last. You know, the lawn mower we've had for the last ten years. I walk behind this lawn mower you bought out of frugality, thinking of things you've said to jar me out of my complacency about life. You've talked about my anger and my distance. The great chasm that lies between us at times. I do think about what you say. At times I wonder how to get you to stop saying those things. At other times I ponder the words alone and think you are right about needing help.

I don't know how to feel or how to express what I feel when I've finally felt it. I'll tell you how I feel. I'm like a big matrushka doll, the kind you pull apart only to find the same thing inside, only smaller. When you get to the middle, it's just a tiny replica of the outer shell. I feel as if I've spent my entire life holding my seam together, because I'm afraid of what might be found at the next layer.

You and others have tried to take the top off my life, and I'm beginning to wonder if I'm not more of a Weeble than a matrushka. I wobble, but I don't fall down, and there seems no way to pull me apart. Maybe I've gone so long living at the surface that I'll never get to another level. But I want to. Somewhere inside I know I don't want to stay the way I am. I desire change. I want to be on the same team with you, not fighting you, neglecting you, or criticizing you. Some of the worst moments of my life are the times just after I've said something, when I know there's no way to take back those words. I watch the words I speak change your face, the lines and creases that signify defeat.

Sometimes I see you with the children and I'm envious. You don't seem to need the trappings of life that I do. I need my work and my position in life to make me feel worthwhile. You feel more fulfilled helping a hurting family or delivering a meal to someone who's sick. I have to be up-front. I have to have recognition. What a charge you get out of simply taking someone's children for the afternoon. I would do that only if I received an award from some ranking official.

I have seen you stand and watch our children playing, even though there are other things you want and need to do. You hold your hand to your mouth, and I have seen you cry as you pour your life into these little ones. You see the horizon, no doubt. You see what will become an empty corner with cobwebs, instead of the Legos that are there in the shape of a farmhouse. I've heard you say, "It just goes by so fast," and I don't comprehend. I don't see the future, because I'm too busy with today. My deadlines. My agenda. I know that in my head. I really do want to change. I want to be more like you in so many ways.

I make fun of your having so many friends, but I know you're much richer for having them. I have my friends. I'm somewhat close with the guys at church. Especially, uh, you know, he lives over in the next subdivision, uh, sits on the right, usually about three rows back. I can't remember his name right now but, oh, you know who I mean. We're pretty close.

You are a professional at relationships. I remember when I first saw pro tennis players practicing and I compared their speed and accuracy with my own. I was in awe. I feel the same about you. The phone rings, and no matter what you're doing you carve out time for friends. You sit with a cup of coffee and cry with someone. This is important to you. I cannot understand why God would do such a wonderful thing as to put you in my life, but he did. I console myself by saying this is the same God who gave me to you, so I'm sure you have some hard questions for him, but I'm thankful.

I tell you that you're not patient enough. I say you need to give me more space. I label your concern as nagging. I hurt you in ways I'll never know. I am more committed to myself than to you, and I recognize it in some flash points of life. The stoplight. Waiting for the kids to get out of school. There are so few times when I don't have tasks on my mind that it's difficult for me to think about such things. But eventually I do, and in those milliseconds of revelation I think of making you more of a priority. But then the light turns green or the children get in the car with muddy shoes, and I'm back to the task at hand.

I used to think that having more would make you happy, would make you content in life. And now I know that is true. But my definition of "more" has changed. You don't want more money or more furniture or more wealth or more attic space. You do want a new light in the kitchen, but that's not really what I'm talking about here. The "more" you want is me, and as yet I've been unable to give it. No excuses. No rationalization. I'm not defending myself on this one. Guilty as charged, I stand.

So I guess I'm really trying to say those words that have eluded my life for so long. I've always prided myself in being correct most of the time. I've always felt that if I stuck with something long enough, like trying to find the right exit off the expressway, I'd get it done, get it right. But there are so many areas where I haven't gotten it right. And it's time to say those words. Actually, it's time to write them.

I'm sorry. Will you forgive me?

I am weak. I truly do not deserve your love. But even if I'm too prideful at times to realize I need it, can you forgive me and start over again with me? Today?

I really am sorry.

Signed in love,

Your HIM

Where there is great love there are always miracles.

WILLA CATHER

Love is the only thing that we can carry with us when we go, and it makes the end so easy.

LOUISA MAY ALCOTT

Many waters cannot quench love; rivers cannot wash it away.

SONG OF SONGS 8:7

Chapter Thirteen

The HIM You've Always Wanted

I have tried to capture the essence of your HIM in the previous twelve chapters. I've tried to show you his foibles as well as those endearing qualities. After all, you fell in love with this man for some reason.

It's probably difficult to remember the exact reason you agreed to love this man for better, for worse. The things you didn't like you overlooked. You magnified the things you did like. Bottom line, you made a commitment before God. You are stuck with a HIM.

Even though he does many dumb things, my guess is that you're not looking for cataclysmic change. You're not looking for perfection, just a little movement in the right direction. A glimmer of hope. After all, if he changed and became perfect, what would that mean for you? Would you really want to live with someone who's perfect? Think of all the things you couldn't say about him with your friends? One of the greatest art forms today is complaints about the husband. And in reality, you know that you can't change your HIM. You can only change yourself.* You cannot manipulate him into becoming a good father, you can't twist his arm into becoming spiritually minded, and you can't be assured that setting a good example before him will make him a godly guy. There's no warranty for a HIM and no service department. The only guarantee anyone can give is that your HIM will remain a HIM until he gets the idea—and it has to be his—that there's more to life than what he's experiencing.

Until my wife came to me, looked me in the eye, got up and turned off the television, came back, woke me up, and looked me in the eye again, I really thought all she wanted was for me to be perfect. I really believed she was looking for performance. Do this, and I'll love you. Do that, and I'll care about you. Vacuum twice a week, and you'll experience passionate romance. Fix dinner once a week and hire a baby-sitter when we go out, and you won't believe what might happen! I thought she wanted SuperHIM, faster than a toddler with diarrhea, able to fold tall mounds of clean laundry.

When she got upset with me for impugning her motives, misinterpreting her statements, or not taking the trash out on time, I set to work to expunge my guilt by cleaning windows, fixing meals, and caring for the children when she didn't expect it. This worked for a while, because I could be SuperHIM for a few hours,* but eventually reality set in, and I realized I could not keep up the pace.

---

*With thanks to every counselor or psychologist I have ever heard or read who says this phrase.

*Actually a few minutes

I went back, in frustration, to my old HIM ways and labeled her as someone who simply expected too much. She was too idealistic. She didn't live in the real world. She didn't want me; she wanted the spirituality of Billy Graham, the tenderness of Mr. Rogers, and the parenting ability of James Dobson.

I was surprised at the realization that my wife did not want all that.

She did not want SuperHIM. What my wife really longed for, and what she had begun the marriage in search of, was relationship. She wanted *us*, not me and her. She wanted us to become one. To cleave. Be soul mates. People on the same team going for the same goal, who didn't have to use word pictures for every little thing. With all my faults and struggles, all of my HIMness, she wanted me. She wanted to go back to the garden. She wanted a little piece of paradise. After all, this is what we were created for in the first place, to have a full, meaningful, enjoyable relationship with the one who created us. An unbridled union between two people created in the image of God captures a bit of the garden every time it's done right, and that's what she wanted.

When I married her, I was looking for a partner. A buddy. Someone to fill that empty space, someone to turn the filmstrip as the beep sounds. In reality I wanted a fabulous cook, a trustworthy nanny, and a passion kitten who would work for the wages of my companionship. That sounds crass, but it's true.

I would be telling you something untrue if I gave the impression that one day she got my attention and everything changed after that.

As I said at the beginning of this book, I am not a counselor, pastor, psychologist, psychiatrist, meteorologist, or marriage mechanic. I am an observer and a reporter. But even reporters get touched by stories they cover every now and then. It's been a long process, and I know I have an awfully long way to go. But there are glimmers of hope in our relationship—more than glimmers. I've made changes, palpable changes, in how I go about relating to her. And if she had not encouraged me to make those changes, I wouldn't have made them.

But my wife did a strange thing to help me accomplish the little movement that has occurred. She left me alone. She stopped working so hard at trying to get me not to "fix" her. She worked on her own life, her own problems. I didn't hear as much about being on the same team. The nagging over the small things ceased. She pulled back from the relationship, and I suddenly felt what it was like to be married to someone like me. She didn't pout. She didn't huff about the house, trying to prove a point. She just went on with her life in this blessed coexistence mode I was used to. As it turned out, it was a mode neither one of us really wanted.

It finally occurred to me that our relationship, this joint venture ordained by God himself, was much more important to me than I realized. It was going to take a lot more work than I expected. It was going to take a lot more time, effort, energy, pain, heartache, struggle, passion, tears, sweat, grocery shopping, walks through the neighborhood, and childbirth classes than I anticipated. I thought marriage was supposed to be easy. I thought commitment was all you needed, and at some point down the road someone threw a big party and patted you on the back for hanging in there all those years. You went riding into the sunset of old age joined by a spiritual hip replacement.

For the first time, the silence of my wife made me hear the deafening roar of regret I faced if I didn't change. Honestly, I still don't have that many close friends, I still do some really dumb things I know I'll regret later, and I'm not as involved with the kids as I'd like to be. But I do have someone who is committed enough to let me experience life at my own pace.

What really changed my heart was when I heard what she had been saying through all the arguments and heartaches over the past few years. She didn't want me to be perfect; she didn't want me to do more; she just wanted *me*. I can live with that. I'm being changed by that kind of love. Your HIM can be, too.

Afterword

For HIMs Only

Hey. How's it goin'? How 'bout those Cubs?

Look, I know how frustrating it is to have someone try to get you to read something. They shove this book under your nose and say, "You'll really like this. It's funny. And there's a chapter just for you."

So I want you to know I feel your pain right now, because I've been there. My wife has, at times . . . excuse me just a moment.

[Hey, women, you can stop reading now. This afterword is for HIM eyes only, okay? You should not be reading this. Thank you.]

Okay, my wife has done this very thing to me, and the express purpose is to get me to change something about myself. "Tell me what you think of this," she'll say. What she means is, "You need to change, and this book tells you how." Well, first of all, I think she ought to keep her books to herself. I don't wave my books in front of her. That's my initial reaction.

[Hey, I said you should stop reading, women! Why are you still reading this? This is only for men. It's top secret stuff, so don't go any farther. Thank you.]

Anyway, I've just spent many pages telling your spouse that I'm glad my wife asked me to change. Ha ha ha. Can you believe that? I said I probably wouldn't have changed if she hadn't in some way moved into my life and created a desire for more depth in our relationship. Ha ha ha ha. Boy, I'll tell you!

Well, that's the reason you're holding this book right now. Your Her not only wants you to experience life to the full, there is something about you she thinks needs tweaking. Perhaps it's your communication. Perhaps she thinks you're a bit angry. Maybe you think more about work than you do your family. Or you think about sex way too much.

I've been in your shoes, pal. I've said the same thing you've said. "You have this impossible standard for me to live up to!" I've said this after she's asked me to keep my side of the bedroom more tidy. I've said this after putting off fixing something around the house that really took only five minutes. I've felt compared to other husbands who seem to have it all together.

I've listened to word picture after word picture. I've heard experts talk about the inner child. I've heard that I need to "get in touch with myself" so much that the next person who says it may need to "get in touch" with a good plastic surgeon.

I've been the cadaver lying on counseling's cold slab. I believed my wife sent all the psychologists to breathe life into me so she would have a real, live human being instead of Frankenstein's emotionally impaired monster.

The startling realization I've come to in the past couple of years is that my wife really, deep down, likes me. She hasn't withheld her love from me, even though she thinks I still have problems. Maybe that describes your relationship with your wife.

I'm not an expert in anything. But I've been around enough guys to know they really want to make their wives happy. Your big desire, as you're driving to and from work, is to walk into a house where your wife is overjoyed to see you, and your children run to you as if you were Barney incarnate. But that doesn't happen too often, does it? Most of the time you get home late, you're upset about something, you take it out on the ones you love, and then you feel crummy about it. You flip on the TV, and three hours later you feel depressed that you just wasted three hours on shows you never intended to watch in the first place.

I know. I've clicked with the best of them. This thing called marriage takes a lot more energy than you thought, right? You're committed. You support your family. You're there when they need you, at least most of the time. But it's just so honkin' hard to hear your wife say, "I need to talk through some important issues," isn't it?

Well, if she's read this book, she now knows not to expect so much from you. She's gained insight into the way you think and what makes you tick, and she knows she should pay more attention when you talk about things that interest you—sports, work stuff.

That play you saw the other night where the quarterback perfectly hid the ball and threw for a touchdown, but the referee blew an inadvertent whistle, so it didn't count. Did you see that?

If you're even the slightest bit open to the possibility that you need to become more involved, if you want to move your marriage up another level, if you want fulfillment and satisfaction, not just from what you do for a living but from the relationships you have, I suggest you do what I did. Listen. Look past her words and the pain on her face and see the heart of a wife who loves you. She really does love you, you know, or she wouldn't have bought this book to try and understand you better. And the startling thing is, you don't have to become "perfect" to please her. She doesn't want perfection; she just wants more of you.

In order to scientifically determine how much change you need, please take the following quiz. (This won't hurt.)

A HIM Quiz

1. Can you name your child's three best friends?
2. Can you name your children?
3. When is your anniversary?
4. Can you remember the month of your anniversary?
5. What is your wife's favorite salad dressing?
6. Have you ever inadvertently told your wife's age to someone?
7. If yes, how long did you spend in the hospital?
8. Do you own a shirt that is more than ten years old?

9. Do you think a great way to end an argument is to have sex?

10. Other than your wife, is there anyone you can approach to talk about things that are really important to you?

There. Wasn't that fun? I think you see my point. There's no need to score this little quiz. But if you see yourself in any of those questions and desire change, if you want to move closer to your wife in a meaningful way, read the following declaration. If you agree with the sentiments written, sign your name at the end. In signing, you are saying you want to change in certain areas and, to the best of your abilities and with God's help, covenant to take specific steps to achieve a greater level of intimacy in your marriage.

May God help you, friend. May God grant you better communication skills, a renewed desire to love your wife and children, and the ability to achieve this without having a lot of books shoved under your nose. I just hate that, don't you?

The Declaration of HIM-Dependence for the Unanimous Declaration of the HOA—HIMs of America

> When in the course of human events, it becomes necessary for a man to dissolve the emotional and financial bonds which have connected him with his parents, and to assume the separate and equal station called marriage, he must lift off the encumbrances of all

dysfunction as a Highly Identifiable Male and impel changes.

We hold these truths to be self-evident, that all men are emotionally impaired, that they are endowed from the beginning with the urge to pursue really neat things that cost a lot of money and are way over budget. We also hold that we are too quick to pick up the newspaper and too slow to change the diaper. We also hold that we have too often thought of our home as our castle and the laundry basket as a basketball hoop, and we have tried far too many three-pointers with our underwear. We also hold that when we have missed, we have failed to rebound or pick up the errant three-pointer. We HIMs seek to eradicate these maladies today and henceforth, for the remainder of this great union.

But we HIMs believe that whenever any force outside of marriage becomes destructive, be it job or hobby, be it the World Series or the play-offs (not including 7th games, of course), it is the right and, yea, duty of the HIM to alter or to abolish that force and to institute a new way of thinking, laying its foundation on such principles as are defined in the Bible and included in books and tapes by Dobson, Smalley, Wright, Chapman, and others, which to them shall seem most likely to effect their spirituality, holiness, and improvement as husbands.

The history of HIMs includes repeated injuries and usurpations by the author of evil himself, all having in direct object the establishment of an absolute tyranny over the Holy One.

We, therefore, the representatives of HIMs of these United States of America, in genuine humility, appealing to the Supreme Judge of the world for the rectitude of our intentions, do, in the Name and by authority of the One who gave himself as a sacrifice for all people, solemnly publish and declare that HIMs are absolved from all allegiance to the minions of Satan; that all connection between us and the legions of hell is and ought to be totally dissolved; that we are free from, not the presence, but the usurpation of sin, having full power to levy war against the enemy of our souls, which is our service forthwith; and that we will do all that is within our power to fulfill the desires of the Holy One, through us, to our wives, children, friends, and relations. And for the support of this Declaration, with a firm reliance on the protection of Divine Providence, we mutually pledge to each other and our Creator, our Lives, our fortunes, and our sacred honor.

Signed _____

Thirty Questions to Bring a HIM and a HER Together

Choose six questions from the following list and discuss them with your spouse. HIMs choose three, HERs choose three. Wives, resist the urge to make your HIM answer all the questions at one sitting. Husbands, resist the urge to say, "I don't know, that's a stupid question." This exercise should take no longer than ten to fifteen minutes, or longer if both parties agree. Repeat this process on another day and continue working through the questions until all have been answered.

1. Describe your feelings when you first met your spouse.
2. What was the best present you ever received from your spouse?
3. What is one thing you take for granted in your spouse?
4. Other than your wedding day, when did your spouse look the most attractive, beautiful, or handsome?
5. What is one thing your spouse does at least once a week that you appreciate?
6. For you, what is a perfect date?

7. Other than the Bible, what book has affected you most in your life? Explain.

8. What film made you think deeply about your life?

9. What color does your spouse look really great in?

10. Describe your most memorable romantic encounter.

11. To which one place in the world would you most like to travel with your spouse?

12. Think about your future. Where would you like to be with your spouse in ten years—what area of the country, how many children, what kind of work, what kind of house, what type of church?

13. What is one thing you'd love to do with your spouse but you've never done because of finances?

14. What is one area where your spouse is smarter or has more ability than you?

15. If you could change one thing about yourself, what would it be?

16. Describe your most embarrassing moment.

17. What aspect of lovemaking do you enjoy the most?

18. Pretend you are stranded on a deserted island with your spouse. What would you absolutely have to do and how would you divide the responsibilities?

19. Now pretend a tribe of cannibals has captured you both and you're about to be eaten (along with a side salad and a baked potato). Other than "I love you," or "HELP!" or "I told you we weren't alone," what would you say to your spouse in those last conscious moments?

20. Try to guess the favorite meal of your spouse including drink, dessert, salad dressing, entrée, and vegetable.

21. What is one area your spouse has grown in since you've been married?

22. What five people from history would you love to invite to dinner? Why did you choose them?

23. Describe the time in your life when you felt most relaxed.

24. If you could become good at something, what would it be (e.g., hobby, sport, ability)?

25. What is your favorite piece of clothing of all time? (HIMs, this is a great chance to tell your wife why you keep that shirt with all the holes in it.)

26. What is the earliest memory you have of your father and mother?

27. What was one fear you had when you were young? Do you still battle that fear today?

28. What is one dream you have for the future?

29. If you could relive one day of your marriage, what day would it be?

30. If you were to die before your spouse, what would you hope he or she would say at your funeral?